My Italian Diary

Other book by the same author
Rush

My Italian Diary

· IAN RUSH ·

With an introduction by
Brian Glanville

ARTHUR BARKER
A division of Weidenfeld (Publishers) Limited
London

To Tracy and Pat – behind every good man ...

Copyright © Ian Rush 1989
Introduction © Brian Glanville 1989

Published in Great Britain by
George Weidenfeld & Nicolson Limited
91 Clapham High Street
London SW4 7TA

ISBN 0 213 16962 2

Printed in Great Britain by
Butler & Tanner Ltd, Frome and London

Contents

Acknowledgements

First and foremost, my thanks go to Ken Gorman of the *Daily Star*. He knows me so well and has done a great job helping me write this book. I am also most grateful to Brian Glanville for supplying the introduction; to Craig Johnston for the 'Italian look' photograph; to my wife Tracy for her chapter; and to Graeme Souness, Kevin Ratcliffe, Jan Molby and my business advisor Paul Dean for their contributions to 'Rush – The Verdict'.

My thanks also go to Steve Hale, who came to see me on several occasions during my year abroad and took many of the photographs for this book. Other photographs are reproduced by kind permission of Action Images, All-Sport, John Dawes (chief sports photographer of the *Daily Star*) and Syndication International Ltd.

Introduction
by Brian Glanville

You might say the writing was on the wall, long before Ian Rush ever got to Turin. Two memories. First, in the sports department of *Il Messaggero*, the Roman daily paper. Lino Cascioli, then the football correspondent, an ebullient, humorous man, his natural good spirits tempered by a fine Roman scepticism, told me, soon after Rush had agreed to join Juventus, 'British footballers never do well in Italy. They'll stick Rush upfield on his own, never give him a decent ball, and when things go wrong, he will be the one they'll blame.' So it transpired.

Liam Brady was almost as pessimistic. In the autumn of 1986, I dined at his apartment in Ascoli, where he had just played against Fiorentina, and was finishing his distinguished Italian career. What worried him, he said, was the question of who would give Rush the ball. Michel Platini, the French international, was definitely leaving Juventus at the end of the season. Who would replace him?

For all the money Juventus spent on transfers during the summer of 1987, the right playmaker for Rush was not produced. No fewer than three different players, be it remembered, cost more than £3 million; Rush himself, a striker called Alessio, from Avellino, who would sink without trace, and an international left-back cum midfielder called De Agostini, from Verona. Then there was the bagatelle of £2.5 million paid out for a pedestrian midfielder called Magrin, from Atalanta of Bergamo, who was awfully good at taking free kicks. Magrin was an unpretentious fellow, who never claimed to be a playmaker, a strategist of genius, the sort of colleague Rush so desperately needed. He, too, would quickly sink into the general morass.

Before Rush took up residence in Piedmont, he was given a taste of the sort of treatment which awaited him; even if it did not go so far as the Italian reporters who encircled him, on one visit, and asked him how Prince Charles was getting on with Di.

It was at a dinner-dance given by an organization called The Juventus Club of London, in a Mayfair hotel, on a summer Saturday night. I was there, and would not have missed it for the world. Time stood still; or grew warped. 'This is an Italy,' said the aghast London correspondent of *La Gazzetta Dello Sport*, 'which in Italy no longer exists.' Rush, as courteous, quiet and uncomplaining as always, was placed, almost symbolically, with his back against the wall, at the long top table. Dinner eaten, a plump Italian in a dinner jacket stationed himself below the bandstand, opposite Rush, across the ballroom floor, and took a microphone. It was clearly to be his finest hour.

'First of all, Ian,' cried Signor Bucci, across the ballroom floor, 'the following season is going to see two big players in Italy. One is you. The other is the Brazilian player, Careca. Two different players. Two different backgrounds. One with a classical Latin-American style; another with a classic Anglo-Saxon style. One's got the technique, the ability of playing with the ball. The other has the ability to score with the left foot, the right foot, the head – in any position.'

Passionate applause.

'I'd like to ask you: which of you two is going to be more successful?'

Rush listens to all this, poker-faced. He replies: 'I think I'm going to the best team in Italy.' Applause. 'We are two completely different players. I shall probably score more goals than him, but he is a very good player. I think Juventus will find it very hard to beat Naples, but I think with the players Juventus have got we can do that, and hopefully win the League.'

Applause.

Signor Bucci resumes. 'You always occupy the attacking position on the field. You never go back to pick up the ball. Journalists from Italy come here and they say, he is always with the front part of the field, and never comes back to help the defence.'

'He's a *striker*!' shouts an affronted small boy.

'I have to score goals,' says Rush, calmly, 'and I don't score goals by going back.'

Signor Bucci insists. 'You are going to play in a completely different kind of football. Different tactics. Different technique. How do you think with such difficulties you're going to score so many goals?'

'I *don't* think I'll score as many goals,' says honest Rush. 'I think that when my team is playing with me, they'll create chances, so hopefully, I'll stay in ratio.' Alas, the hope would be dashed. They wouldn't, nor would he.

Signor Bucci again, irrepressible: and oh how prescient! 'You're probably going to miss Platini!' he cries, 'because you're not going to receive as many balls from Laudrup!'

How true. Michael Laudrup, the young Dane, expected not only to make chances for Rush but to play Virgil to his Dante, interpret for him, smooth his path, facilitate his difficult transition, would do little or nothing of the sort. He himself would have a shocking season, scoring not a single goal and, far from helping Rush, there was the impression he seemed almost to resent him. The following season, when Juventus arranged to sign the Russian midfielder Alexander Zavarov, a foreigner had to go. Laudrup seemed the obvious choice, but Laudrup has a father called Finn, once a Danish international himself, agent for his son and a bitterly hard bargainer, who demanded the earth, the last lira, were his son to move on to PSV Eindhoven. Juventus capitulated, Laudrup stayed, Rush came home; and Laudrup, with such players as Zavarov and Rui Barros of Portugal beside him, has gone on to score and to flourish, again.

What, though, did Rush reply to the insistent Signor Bucci. Patient, tolerant, courteous, long-suffering, before this bombardment of Chico Marxism, he said, 'I think Platini and Laudrup are two completely different styles of player. Platini is a great player, but I'm looking forward to playing with Laudrup. I think we'll do very well together.' They didn't.

As we know now, almost everything went wrong. With the advantage of hindsight, it is difficult to see how it could have been otherwise. To what extent did Rush's own, introverted, personality contribute to the fiasco? Only, I would say, so far as it compounded the bleak situation on the field. If Rush had had Zavarov and Rui Barros, or their like, beside him, if he had had a Platini, he would assuredly have gone on getting goals, everybody would have loved him, and he and they would have lived happily ever after. Instead, everything went quickly to pot, and the fact that Rush is a shy young man, never wholly happy outside the confines of Anfield and his supportive community in Flint, exacerbated matters.

Comparisons with that other Welsh international centre-forward, John Charles, King John, who had scored over ninety goals for Juventus after joining them from Leeds

United in 1957, were not just odious, they were profoundly irrelevant. Ian was from North Wales, John was an extrovert, genial, jolly Swansea man. Ian came into a largely untried team at a transitional period for the club. John found on his right Giampiero Boniperti, then captain of Italy, by now President of Juventus, and on his left, Omar Sivori, the brilliant little Argentine international, newly arrived from Buenos Aires. Juventus won the Championship straight off.

I twice went to see Rush in Italy, the first time in the autumn in Verona, where Juventus were beaten 2–1. Peeping afterwards through the dressing-room door, I saw him sitting on the bench, head bowed, the picture of melancholy. So little had he been given the ball during the ninety minutes that one leading Italian sports paper would not even give him the usual mark out of ten. Generously and objectively enough, the Italian press apportioned no blame to Rush. They appreciated that the team he had to play with simply could not give him the kind of service he wanted.

Of course, as results continued to be poor, things grew more and more sour. Graeme Souness, once a sturdy support for Rush at Liverpool, later a success with Sampdoria of Genoa, was heard to say he doubted whether Ian would ever settle down, away from his family and friends in Flint, doubted if he would ever manage to learn Italian. Again, that wouldn't have mattered, had the team been better assembled, had the goals gone in.

When I returned to Italy in November, the romance between Rush and Juventus was manifestly dead. A word or two about the Juventus club might be appropriate here. It has long been virtually the fief of the Agnelli family, the enormously wealthy and immensely influential owners of Fiat, and of so much more. Gianni Agnelli, the boss of Fiat, is also very much the boss of Juventus, though his nominal role is merely honorary. The whole sparkling career of Giampiero Boniperti, at least since his retirement from the field, has been owed to Agnelli. President he may have been for years but it is still Agnelli, known as *l'avvocato*, the lawyer, who calls the shots, Agnelli on whose every word – often provocative and feckless – reporters fawn, at every match he attends. Agnelli's interventions don't always turn out for the best. For example, the period in which he was forever needling Zibi Boniek, the Polish star, who seemed to play so much better in European floodlit games than in the Championship that Agnelli nicknamed him, 'Bello di Notte', Nighttime Beauty, a play on the title of the Bunuel film, *Belle de Jour*, Daytime Beauty. Boniek left, went to Roma, flourished; and Juventus missed him.

There is no doubt in my mind that Agnelli could have waved his wand, said the magic word, and saved Rush from all that happened; at least within the club. 'I have the training,' he suddenly burst out, at dinner in Turin. 'I'm like an outcast.' Obviously not a remark one could report at the time, but deeply indicative. But Agnelli was plainly looking for another Platini, another sophisticated fellow who could entertain him and amuse him, a courtier. Ian Rush was never going to be that.

On the day I had dinner in Turin with Rush, I had lunch in Pisa with Paul Elliott, the accomplished black centre-half who had been surprisingly bought by Pisa from Aston Villa in the summer of 1987; and did surprisingly well. Lately, Elliott had had an excellent game in Pisa against Rush and Juventus, though Juventus had won at the last 2–1, with a shot by Rush which went in off Elliott's leg, Elliott having previously scored a spectacular goal, himself. Elliott said he admired Rush but didn't envy him. A loyal team-mate, Tacconi, the garrulous Juventus goalkeeper, had just said that Rush was a £3.5 million misfit.

Elliott put it very differently. 'I've come here in a silent way. Rushie came here with all chariots blazing and all guns firing. They think he's the greatest thing since sliced bread. If he scores a goal, he's a hero, if he doesn't, he's a villain, whereas if I score, everybody goes mad.' Elliott thought Rush had played very well against Pisa, taking up all sorts of good positions, but seldom getting the ball. 'He made some terrific runs between me and the sweeper. He's a very intelligent player, you know. Everywhere he goes, they're playing to the opposite side. I could see it happening. When he gets the ball, Laudrup's twenty metres to his left, Alessio is thirty metres to his right. You're very happy, because all he can do then is play it back, again: he has me and the sweeper against him.'

I shall pass over the infinite, silly squabbles over Rush's 'failure' time and again to return punctually from Britain, when he had permission to return home; of the times he was quoted out of turn. An unhappy episode, but at least he didn't emerge from it the poorer ... financially anyway.

· ONE ·

Arrivederci, Anfield

The waiting is nearly over now. And I just want to go. I've had a year to think about it, to prepare my mind, to focus all my thoughts. It's been too long, really.

God, is it really a year since I went over to Turin and signed for Juventus? In some ways it seems an age ago . . . but that's because so much has happened this past twelve months. Really, the time has flown by, even more quickly than the plane I'm waiting for now which will transport Tracy and myself to our new life in Italy.

Just think, a couple of hours and I'll be over in Turin again, this time for good – well, for three years at least – I hope! But what if I'm the biggest flop ever to hit Italian football, what if the goals dry up? They have invested well over £4 million in me when you add my wages to the £3.2 million they have paid Liverpool.

Being a flop is no more than a quickly-passing fear though. I'm not really frightened of the challenge ahead. I'm nervous, a bit keyed up, but that's what you expect to feel. It's the kind of feeling you get before every big match – and I hope there are a lot of big matches to come for Juventus.

Basically I'm still a bit shy, so it will be a bit of an ordeal meeting all those new faces, all my new team-mates. But I do have a lot of confidence in my own ability. I've proved I can score goals, in England anyway. I know that goals in Italy are going to be a lot harder to come by, with so much emphasis on defensive football over there. But you can only do your best.

It was so different seven years ago, when I was preparing to begin my life with Liverpool. I'd cost £350,000 then, making me Britain's most expensive teenager. But Anfield seemed so big and so grand after Chester I was scared of the other players because they were such big names.

My first six months at Liverpool were the most miserable of my life. I'd just tip-toe into the changing room, get myself in a corner and not say a word. Because I was so shy in those days, I took some terrible stick from the other lads. For what seemed an eternity I used to think they had something against me. Then I gradually learned that mickey-taking was – and still is – a way of life at Anfield.

Right now, I reckon it's the dressing room banter that I'll miss more than anything. The lads at Liverpool reckoned they could hear me coming half way down the corridor, I loved arriving for training, all the cracks and the jokes.

I guess I'll have to sit there like a dummy again in the Juventus dressing room, for the first few months at least. They'll be cracking jokes and I won't be able to understand them! It's the language problem that bothers me more than anything else. I can hardly speak English that well, never mind a foreign language like Italian!

I started learning the language – or trying to – back in January. I used to play language cassettes in my car, but it might have been double Dutch to me. Tracy started a couple of months earlier and she's fluent already. I ought to feel a bit ashamed of myself but the fact is that she's a much better person than me, she's far more intelligent.

She left school with a batch of O Levels and got a job in a bank. All I left with was an ear-bashing from the headmaster that I should have worked harder. If I hadn't happened to have a bit of ability as a footballer, I don't know what I'd be doing now – probably on the dole.

It's great having Tracy with me. We've only been married for seventeen days but she's been a vital part of my life since I was a teenager with Chester. She comes from Flint, like me, but strangely we'd never met before she saw me drunk in a disco more than six years ago.

She's been the only serious girl in my life ever since. And I know how important a part she will play over the next three years. Mark Hughes, my striking partner in the Welsh team, is a good pal of mine and we chatted about his move to Barcelona a year ago. He struggled over there in his first season – and he's a great player.

Strangely enough, I think his problems will help me. He said he had two main problems – the language and being over in Spain on his own. When you don't have a partner to talk to and things are going wrong, it can't be much fun having to go back to your apartment, however luxurious, and stare at the four walls. But I'm certain he'll do better this year. He married his girlfriend Jill a week earlier than Tracy and I were wed, and he knows, now, what to expect over there.

We're planning to have Italian lessons every week in our apartment. But while I'm still a novice at the lingo, I'll have to be careful not to make the mistake Jan Molby did when he joined Liverpool. The form of English he was taught by the lads included every swearword in the book! I reckon the lads at Juventus will be working out similar words for me to say to referees!

Jan Molby ... now there's a name to conjure with. He's an amazing character, a real powerhouse on the field but a guy who likes the odd night out from time to time. Let's be honest, most of us always did at Liverpool. Apart from being the best team in Europe I'll bet we were always the most sociable, too.

The boss, Kenny Dalglish, followed in the tradition of all the other managers at Anfield in treating the players like adults, allowing them time to enjoy themselves when the time was right. I'm one of the lucky ones. I haven't trained properly for some ten weeks now since the last season ended in England. I've had a lot to eat and a fair bit to drink in that time and I'm a couple of pounds lighter than I was back in May. I always lost weight in the summer, then built up my muscles in pre-season training to put it back on.

I pulled on Liverpool's number nine shirt for the last time, in Tel Aviv against the Israeli national side. We were hammered 3–0 as well! Not the most memorable way to end seven fantastic years, but I don't really class that as my farewell to Liverpool. Nor even my last game in England, even though I scored in our 3–3 draw at Chelsea.

For me, the emotional and almost spiritual farewell to my beloved Liverpool came in our last home game of the season, against Watford on Easter Monday. That was my last appearance at Anfield and I'm not ashamed to say it ended in tears.

I'd known right from the start of the season that I had a battle to win with the Kop. Remember that I had already signed for Juventus and was just leased out to Liverpool for the season. I knew that some of our fans would believe that I would do no more than go through the motions. I had been told that the old hero of Anfield, Kevin Keegan, had been given a pretty rough reception after he had announced he was quitting the club to seek his future abroad. I just didn't want that to happen to me.

But I scored in the Charity Shield at Wembley, then I got two more as we opened the season with a 2–0 win at Newcastle. I think the fans realized then that I was going to give everything and they responded to me. I've got an awful lot to thank our supporters for as they really helped me through last season.

In fact, I reckon it was my best season ever. I scored forty goals, which isn't my best total, but I believe I've become a better all-round player. It's the only season in which I played in every single game – even in friendly matches I played at least half a game. So I was hoping that the crowd would give me a warm goodbye against Watford, but I wasn't ready for the kind of scenes I witnessed that day.

There were a lot of our supporters waiting outside the players' entrance to give me a cheer as I walked in. Then, about forty minutes before the kick-off Kenny came over and asked me if I'd like to be captain for the day. I took some terrible stick from Molby, Steve McMahon and Ronnie Whelan – probably my three biggest mates – but I was really proud leading them all out.

The game itself wasn't the most spectacular of the season. Watford battled hard to contain us and with seven minutes to go it was still 0–0. Then a long ball was played through their defence, I just ran onto it and touched it past Steve Sherwood and into the net. I suppose I've scored a hundred like it – but the Kop exploded. I just felt relief . . . I'd have hated my last game to finish goalless.

But just about everybody in the packed ground kept chanting my name right up to the final whistle. And when the game was over, the noise grew even louder. I did a lap of honour right round the ground, all on my own. The supporters I could see were all in tears, all trying to hand me their scarves and their hats. I was amazed, I kept wondering: 'Why are they doing all this for me?' Then I touched my face and realized there were tears running down my cheeks too. As a spontaneous gesture back, I suddenly found myself pulling off my shirt and tossing it into the crowd. It caused a right scramble and I gather that the lad who finally grabbed it had to have a police escort out of the ground!

These were the most moving moments of my whole life. I've seen players leaving Liverpool before and the fans have just accepted it. But this was fantastic. My dad was sat up in the stand and the man next to him told him: 'I've been coming to Liverpool for thirty years and I've never seen anything like this before.'

I was overwhelmed by the time I reached the tunnel, where the players from both teams had waited for me. It was a nice gesture by the Watford lads to all shake my hand before leaving the pitch. Back in the dressing room I was presented with the matchball, signed by all our players. Some nice remarks, too. McMahon wrote: 'You won't be missed'. Mark Lawrenson wrote: 'Ciau'. And some joker signed: 'All the best, Luigi!'

An hour after the game there were still around five thousand fans outside the ground, waiting for me. I wanted to go and give them a final wave but the police said it would be too dangerous. They were worried about people getting hurt in a stampede. So they had to smuggle me out, across the pitch and through the far entrance, while somebody went and brought my car. What a way to go!

Maybe the whole afternoon was best captured by one supporter, a chap called John Duffy, who came to me inside the ground to ask for my autograph. He was so moved he could hardly speak. 'All the best for the future, Ian lad, you've brought a lot of happiness into my life,' he managed to say. 'Remember that one you scored at Brighton? I'll never forget you and I hope you're every bit as successful over there.'

All I could say in reply was 'Ta!' But it wasn't because that was all I felt. I could have broken down and cried with John there and then.

Mind, I was feeling a little bit low because I'd invited all the other players to bring their wives out for a meal at Churchill's, a well-known restaurant in Liverpool. But, apart from Ronnie Whelan, they all said no, they made excuses. I was calling them all a right miserable bunch, under my breath, I tell you.

So Ronnie, myself and the two girls went as a foursome only for me to discover when we arrived that the whole team had got there before me. They had arranged a big party for me and kept it secret. That was so typical of the lads, it left me really choked. There can't be a better bunch of footballers anywhere else in the world.

At the end of it all, though, I thought of the words Joe Fagan had said to me some hours earlier. I had gone into the bootroom to say my goodbyes to all the backroom staff. I wanted to see Joe in particular, he's a really nice man who had been especially kind to me when he had been manager.

He pulled me to one side and told me: 'Son, don't ever look back. You've had a fabulous time here, you've enjoyed it and given a lot of people pleasure. But that's all over now, you've got to look forward. If you look back, you'll only make yourself miserable.' Strangely I'd been told much the same thing by Alan Oakes, the manager at Chester, when I left them to join Liverpool. I know it's good sound advice so I'm determined to take it.

Chelsea made me a presentation before the game there, which I thought was nice of them. Their chairman Ken Bates and striker Kerry Dixon gave me a big bottle of wine – Italian, of course – and a huge stick of celery! I couldn't quite understand the latter gift – but I know that the fans on their shed, though they clapped me beforehand, gave me plenty of stick once the game got underway.

John Aldridge, the striker Liverpool signed to take my place, made my goal at Stamford Bridge, putting me through six yards out. I was pleased to make one back for him later. He's a good lad, Aldo, a Scouser through and through and he'll get a lot of goals for them after I've gone, I'm sure of that. People say he looks like me and plays like me. Well, I take that as a compliment – the second part, anyway!

We went straight from Chelsea to Heathrow, for that game against Israel I've mentioned before. To be fair it was more of a holiday break for the lads after a tough season. We'd all had a good bit to drink and we didn't do ourselves anything near justice. In fact we were three down before we'd kicked a ball.

I was wound up like mad because a local journalist whose newspaper had organized the trip promised me £2,000 if I could score twice. But I reckon I was trying too hard, if anything, running round like a lunatic instead of playing my normal game. Our coach Ronnie Moran, who would play a game of scrabble as if his life depended on it, had a right go at us at half time: 'You're playing for Liverpool now, you should feel ashamed of yourselves for letting down that red shirt,' he stormed at us.

We did take heed of his words, battling a lot better in the second half. If we'd scored one we'd have got three. But we just couldn't get that break. My only sadness as I took off the Liverpool shirt for the last time afterwards was at finally having to say goodbye to all the lads.

My big disappointment as far as the fans were concerned was that I hadn't been able to help win a trophy for them in my last season. In many ways, the ideal time to have left would have been a year earlier when we achieved that fabulous double of the First Division Championship and the FA Cup. This time we lost the title to Everton after being nine points clear at one stage. And we lost the League Cup final 2–1 to Arsenal after opening the scoring.

It's difficult to know why we blew the League. We had such a spectacular run in mid-season then we just seemed to fade. That's not like Liverpool at all, we were always renowned for coming on strong at the end of a season. Maybe a bit of complacency had crept in because we seemed to be in such an uncatchable position. I just don't know.

What made it all the more galling was that we honestly felt we were the best team in the country, better than Everton. We played them five times all told that season and they never beat us once. We hammered them three times and drew twice. Yet they won the League. And while at least it was my big pal in the Welsh team Kevin Ratcliffe who received the trophy as Everton's captain, I'm sure that even he wouldn't claim that they were a better side than us.

The League Cup was another let down, especially for me. Because it was the first time in all my years at Liverpool that I'd scored and finished on a losing team. My record had lasted for well over one hundred games. And, while players as a rule are not as interested in statistics as the supporters and the newspapers, there was a certain psychological advantage for us.

If I got a goal, I'm sure that players on the opposing team, remembering the record, must have felt it was not going to be their day. And I reckon it acted as a tonic to my own team-mates. It was a bitter feeling, walking off Wembley with nothing. All the more so because we had been so much on top in that first hour I thought we'd win by three or four.

Then Charlie Nicholas struck with a lucky deflection and the game left us from there. So we had nowt to show at the end of the season unless you count the Super Cup we won by beating Everton. To finish second in the League and reach Wembley might constitute a great season for some clubs. At

Liverpool, because of the standards we had set ourselves, it was failure and it inevitably provoked speculation that things were not well under Kenny Dalglish.

Some people saw my leaving as the beginning of a break up of the team. My only answer to that is: Rubbish! Liverpool will get things right again next season, and just watch. If they don't win the title then the team which finishes above them will.

Dalglish has already shown his determination to keep the club at the top by spending the money he got for me on Peter Beardsley and John Barnes. They are both enormously gifted footballers. And along with Aldridge they'll make up one hell of an attacking force. I met the new boys a couple of days ago and while Beardsley seems a quiet sort of fellow I was hugely amused by Barnes.

He is, I believe, the first black player Liverpool have ever bought and there was some speculation about how the fans on Merseyside would take to him. But he showed he has the right sense of humour for the task. 'I'm just here to bring some colour to the team,' he told me.

I'd been in to train with the players after meeting Dalglish the previous day when I went to Anfield to collect my boots. I'd asked him then if it would be all right to come in for just a couple of hours work, to give myself at least a start before I began with Juventus. 'No problem,' he said. He told me I was welcome to come and train there any time, even if I was home playing for Wales. It's a warm feeling to know you're not just gone and forgotten.

Mind, I learned my place. The first team had a practice game against the reserves that morning. So I trained with the kids! Still, I reckon I at least blew away some of the cobwebs of the last nine or ten weeks ... and what a close season I had to recover from. . . .

From the time I walked off the pitch at Chelsea I seem to

have spent my life in planes, airports, in church – and in the nick! It's been a fantastic roller coaster summer with that trip to Israel followed by a five-day break in Spain with a few team-mates, then a holiday with Tracy in Mauritius, a trip to Turin to find ourselves a home, a four-day trek to Sweden on behalf of Nike, my boot sponsors, and finally a honeymoon on a paradise island in the Dutch Indies called Aruba.

Every trip provided its own store of memories but I'll tell you of two in particular. Our visit to Italy was supposed to be a private affair, a chance for Tracy and myself to choose an apartment to rent. We found our own fairytale palace, which I'll tell you about later.

But what really sticks in my mind was the press conference we had to give to Italian journalists, once they had discovered we were coming. I didn't mind, because I know that learning to deal with the press will be one of my major tasks in Italy. Yet I wasn't quite prepared for some of the questions they were to ask and I didn't really have the answers, either.

'What about the marriage?' one asked me. Only he wasn't referring to Tracy and me – he wanted my views on Prince Charles and Princess Diana! Then they wanted my opinion on Mrs Thatcher, on Italian literature, religion, even on Italian food. You obviously need to take a degree at the Open University before coming to Juventus!

I had been warned in advance to choose my answers carefully, to be as non-committal as possible because some of the reporters over there will murder you with an unguarded quote, taken completely out of context. So when they asked me about the problems allegedly besetting the royal couple I said: 'I don't know really, it's a while since I've spoken to them!'

One asked me if I would have enlisted to fight in the Falklands war if I'd been asked. My reply: 'I'd go anywhere for a game of football!' Would I rather work for Mrs Thatcher or Mr Boniperti? 'I don't think Mrs Thatcher has a football team . . .'.

When Platini was here he had a Ferrari, was I disappointed because I hadn't been given one? 'No, I'm just a new boy here and I don't deserve one yet. I've got to prove myself first and try to become the success Michel Platini was.'

The papers in Turin, the kinder ones anyway, have christened me The Eagle. But one reporter wasn't so generous. He likened me, facially, as 'a cross between Charlie Chaplin and Adolf Hitler'! Tracy didn't come out of it too well, either. She had sat in on the press conference, sipping a glass of Coca Cola. She was shocked to discover that by the time the papers hit the streets she'd been knocking back Campari! A comic-dictator and a dipso ... we obviously make a fine couple!

Mind, we almost didn't make a couple at all en route to our honeymoon. We'd had a fabulous wedding at my local Catholic church in Flint and reception at the magnificent Ruthin Castle. Ronnie Whelan was my best man – his speech was even worse than mine – and all the lads still in England were there among three hundred guests.

Maybe I was on too much of a high when we set off for Aruba. But I took the wrong passport. Like many footballers I have two because if your job takes you to Israel and your passport is stamped there it will no longer be accepted in many of the Arab countries. I took the passport which did not have my visa for entering the United States.

We had to land at Miami to change planes. And I was promptly arrested when the passport official at the airport found I did not have that visa. I was frogmarched to a shack well away from the main terminal, where I was herded into a room with a bunch of other 'criminals'. There was an armed guard on the door, to make sure nobody tried to escape.

For some three hours I was kept there and I was beginning to get just a little bit nervous by the time I was finally marched out again and told I could continue on my journey. I know it was my mistake in the first place, but I couldn't help thinking that they had come on a bit strong in their reaction.

It didn't spoil the honeymoon! We had a marvellous time on one of the most beautiful islands in the world. There was barely a person who could speak English, and there was just one waiter who recognized me. I also telephoned Paul Dean, who acts as my adviser, to see if he could help smooth things out at Miami on the return journey – the security people were much more considerate this time. We still had to wait a few hours, but we were allowed to stay in a comfortable room and Tracy was allowed to remain with me.

'Al Italia announce the departure of their flight to Turin...' Well, I guess it's time to go. Tracy and I have been sat in the departure lounge for the past hour or so, along with all the thousands of other people waiting to wing their way across the world. I don't consider myself a superstar and I don't especially enjoy the trappings of stardom ... but it would still have been nice to have all this part smoothed out a bit, to be travelling first-class or club-class rather than economy-class.

Somebody told me that Diego Maradona has his own private plane, to fly him and his team of five or six full-time assistants on his travels. Now I'm not putting myself in his class – he's the best in the world. But here am I, who did cost a few bob, with a cheap ticket ... and my 'staff' consists of Paul Dean, who doubles between acting as my unofficial agent and his principal job, working for a Trust Company and an accountant, Colin Hall, who numbers me among his clients. Some superstar....

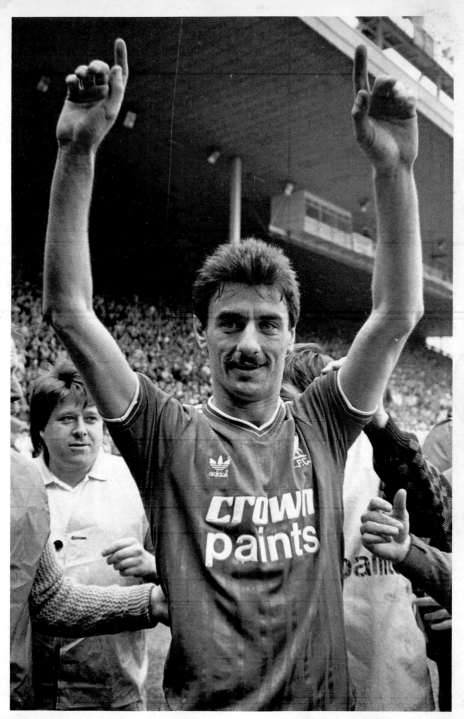

Thanks for the memories . . . what I thought was my final game at Anfield.

Last strike for the fans – the goal that beat Watford.

Goodbye to the lads in the boot room . . .

. . . but farewell is a lonely sound.

A busy summer. Getting wed . . .

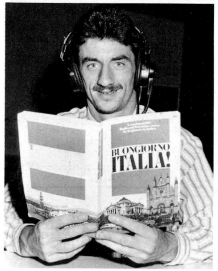

. . . and trying to learn a new language.

The Italian look – as created by Anfield's own photographer, Craig Johnston.

Mobbed on arrival in Turin. What have I let myself in for?

I find some peace and quiet at our ground.

'No, I don't know Prince Charles personally.' My first meeting with the Italian press.

In the arcade with some of my junior fan club.

It's not much, but it's home.

Tracey and me in the gardens . . .

... bet she won't head this one.

A sightseeing trip in Turin.

With my Juventus team-mates (left to right) back row: Favero, Laudrup, Bruno, Brio and Tacconi; front row: Scirea, Vignola, Bonini, Alessio, Magrin.

A 'Zebra' in flight.

· TWO ·

La Dolce Vita?

I've just pulled on the Juventus number nine shirt for the first time and marked my debut with a goal! That makes a change. It took me eight games to get my first goal for Liverpool and as many to notch my first for Wales.

It was the opening goal in our 2–0 win over Lucerne in a friendly arranged to end our ten days' pre-season training here. It was a simple enough affair ... I just moved first to meet a free kick and touched over their goalkeeper as he came out to me. Marino Magrin, another of our new players, scored the second from a penalty.

So professionally I'm feeling quite satisfied as I pack up my clothes ready for the four-hour coach drive back to Turin. Yet I'd be lying if I said I was totally happy. It's been a lonely ten days for me in some ways and it's all caused by the language barrier.

It would be unfair to lay the blame on my new team-mates. I knew when I came that the spirit in any other club in the world could never equal Liverpool's. A few of the Juventus players have been as friendly and helpful as they can, doing

29

their best to make me feel at home. And when you remember that we have six newcomers to the squad all told, it's going to take time for all of us to settle. I do realize that.

But I just feel out of things when the dressing room banter starts. It's a bit like my early days at Liverpool, I just sit there and say little ... and realize I should have worked harder at learning Italian before I came out. In England I kept saying to myself: I'll worry about it when I get there. Now I realize I should have done it months ago.

Of course it's too late by then. I guess I'm just a very lazy person, one that gets easily downhearted. I've been telling myself already that I'll never learn the language. And that's ridiculous. I get frustrated because I can't talk like a native after a week!

When I look at it seriously, I realize that it must take time. Michael Laudrup, the Danish international who is my striking partner and my new room-mate, told me it took him four or five months before he could even begin to hold a conversation. Mark Hateley has said he was still struggling after a couple of years!

Laudrup's a good mate. He can speak English as well as I can so he has filled me in with all the rules and regulations as much as he can. But I can't spend all my life on his shoulder, he has to get on with his own affairs.

I met my new colleagues for the first time when we got together at the Stadio Comunale – the ground Juventus share with their arch-rivals Torino – in readiness for our trip to Switzerland. I recognized people like Antonio Cabrini, Sergio Brio, Massimo Bonini and Gaetano Scirea immediately. I had faced them in that tragic European Cup final at Heysel a couple of years earlier.

Indeed Brio had marked me and I knew what a good player he was. He gave me barely an inch, yet he was scrupulously fair, he never resorted to kicking you. I did take some stick

in that game but it was from Tardelli who's left the club now
... maybe just as well!

Juventus had signed six new players all told, in a £10
million summer spending spree. Apart from myself, who cost
them £3.2 million, they had spent £5 million on Luigi De
Agostini and Roberto Tricella, two Italian internationals
they bought from Verona. They also spent smaller amounts
on Angelo Alessio (from Avelino), Pasquale Bruno (Como)
and Marino Magrin (Atalanta).

There seemed to be thousands of fans at the ground to
watch us all arrive and then leave. I was driven to the ground
by a man called Allasio Lucca, who owns the apartment we
are renting. There was such a crush of people around the car
that poor Mr Lucca found several dents and scratches where
people had been trying to break the doors open! It was a
foretaste, I guess, of the fever of the fans in this country.

Rino Marchesi, Juventus' team manager, joined the six
new players for pictures from the horde of press photographers. He's a well-known and highly-rated manager in
Italy, having worked at Napoli and Inter Milan. It's his
second year with Juve but he's under some pressure. The
club didn't win anything last season. And while finishing
runners up to Napoli in the First Division might be regarded
as successful by some clubs, it's just not good enough for a
club like ours.

Mr Marchesi reminds me of an English gentleman. He
really is a very nice, warm man who can speak a little English
... at least enough to get by on. But he likes to talk to me in
Italian, to see if I have been learning. That just adds to the
frustration for me.

I found the ten-day training programme in Switzerland a
bit difficult, because I'd just had the longest close-season
break since I started playing football. Physically, it probably
wasn't as hard as the pre-season training I knew from my

Liverpool days. But it was a vastly different routine.

At Liverpool, the early work at our training ground was all about building up stamina, physical strength and durability for the season ahead. Then we'd head off abroad somewhere, to play anything up to half a dozen friendly games to get the football side of our training up to scratch.

Here we've had less concentration on stamina and more on things like stretching exercises. I just wasn't used to it . . . and I was left with some aching muscles! There was a lot of work on practising ball skills as well. In fact I was surprised at the sheer technical abilities of all the players, technically they are better over here.

But that's not to say that Juventus would beat Liverpool. My old club would have an edge in physical strength. Maybe they need that because they have to play forty league games a season, while in the Italian First Division it's only thirty. With cup ties and the like, a lot of English players will have to throw themselves into combat up to sixty times in a season and that's too much.

I'm like most players inasmuch as I'd much prefer to be playing than training. But the two games a week schedule we used to have at Liverpool, especially when we were in Europe, takes its toll on bodies. By the time Christmas has come and gone players begin to get physically tired and mentally jaded. Then they pick up little niggling injuries and continue to play when they're not fully fit – and they lose their sharpness.

I had another eye-opener about the fanaticism of the Juventus fans when several thousand of them turned up at the weekend just to watch us train. And when we played Lucerne there must have been around 16,000 at the stadium half of them wearing our colours. I was pleased by their cheers and chanting when I scored but even more so when all the other players shook my hand. I was dying to show them that I could score goals.

Incidentally, I gather I've already won one award, even before the season is near to starting. Fifty of Italy's top coaches voted me the best buy of the season. I only hope they're still thinking that in nine months time!

SUNDAY 16 AUGUST: GENOA

So this is what la dolce vita, the sweet life, is all about! The Juventus team coach has just been attacked by a howling mob of rival fans as we arrived here for a 'friendly'. There were hundreds of young hooligans throwing plastic bottles at the bus and chanting and shoving the bus as we arrived at the ground.

We all crouched down inside the coach, just in case any windows were smashed. But fortunately the local riot police, with their dogs, managed to break up the mob before they could do us any real harm. It was a nasty few minutes though, the kind of violence we seem to have stamped out of the game back in England.

All the players were warned when we reached the safety of the dressing room not to talk about the incident to the press. Juventus are very conscious of their image, they do not like to be involved in anything they consider to be unsavoury.

Players can be fined – and heavily – for talking out of turn to the newspapers. If a player came out and said he wanted a move, for example, he would be whacked in his next pay packet. In fact it has happened already this season to one player, so a journalist told me. All he had said was that he was unhappy at losing his place to one of the new signings!

Anyway, I hit back at those fans in the best way possible ... by scoring the quickest goal of my career. It came after just thirty seconds and we added another to win the game

2–0. I was pleased because it kept up my record of scoring in every friendly game so far. I'd managed eight so far in five games, including a hat-trick in a match between the first team and the reserves.

It wasn't just a kickabout, either. It was the kind of fixture they used to play in England before the start of a season. We played up at a peaceful little hamlet called Villar Perosa, some twenty-five miles from Turin and nestling in the foothills of the Italian Alps. This was my first trip to a setting that was to become an important part of my life, because it's where Juventus take their players on the day before every home game.

The hotel is not palatial but it is bright and clean, the food is first-class and the staff will do absolutely anything to make you comfortable. There's a small games room with a bar billiards table and out on the verandah there's one of those football games where you turn the handles to make the players move.

It has been chosen by the club for our hideaway because it is normally so quiet and peaceful. But on the day we played our game on the adjacent football field about 8,000 fans came up. They were all allowed into the hotel to speak to us, collect autographs and take pictures. But once the season starts for real, I'm told they will be kept well away. This is where we need to relax before our games.

The senior team won the game 5–0 . . . but I finished with a few bruises from where the reserve players had tried to make their mark! The fans gave me a great reception when I scored my goals and at the final whistle there was a pitch invasion, with hundreds of them mobbing me all the way back to the hotel, where we changed.

So far at least, our own fans have been wonderful towards me. I've had the odd one come up in the street and touch me, just to see if I'm real! But I've had no aggro from any of them, they're just so excited about the coming season. It did cross the back of my mind that there would be the occasional one who might remember Heysel ... but the only people who have mentioned it are those who have come over from England to see me.

MONDAY 17 AUGUST: THE WELSH HARP, FLINT

Here I am, back among my own folk just for the night. Juventus have let me come back home for a couple of days to organize the moving of some furniture from Wales to our new apartment and to sort out one or two business affairs. It's nice to see the lads again, to enjoy a conversation in a language I can understand!

But Tracy and myself are back over in Turin tomorrow. Although we've found an apartment that suits us both, we can't move in until September because we can't get the furniture for it until then. Every major department store in Turin closes down for August, which means we can't buy a thing until September.

We're both dying to move in there because it's an absolute dream of a place. It's high on the hillside, barely a mile from the bustling city centre yet it's a different world. We have rented the top floor of a seventeenth-century mansion. It has three bedrooms, three bathrooms, a lovely kitchen and living room and a spare room we can convert into a games room.

The gardens outside are luxurious enough for a castle, with peach trees, grapevines, roses ... all a bit different from downtown Flint where I was born. It also has first-class security – gates that you can only open by remote control! The owner, Mr Lucca, lives with his family on the ground floor.

My only reservation is that it's a bit pricy, but we have taken out a six months' lease with the option of staying if we're still happy. Right now, we'll just be happy to move in. Mind, Juventus have put us up in a smashing little hotel called the Sitea.

Its address, would you believe, is Via Carlo Alberto ... although I'm not sure it wasn't around for years before the Brazilian captain lifted the World Cup back in 1970. The staff there have all been as kind and friendly as you could wish. But it will be nice to be settled into a home of our own.

· THREE ·

Flying Low

It had to happen! My first competitive game for Juventus and I finish up without a goal and carrying a thigh injury. I'd scored two more goals in our last friendly game three days previously, taking my tally to ten in just six games. It had been too good to last.

Before my earlier games the fans had been saying 'One goal today!' to me. But I guess they had been spoiled as I had by the way the goals kept flowing. We played at Lecce in our first Italian Cup tie, with four more to follow before the League season was due to begin. There were hordes of Juve supporters among the 30,000 crowd at the stadium and some of them were coming up and demanding, 'Two, three goals today!'

I was a bit wary, because I knew that my record so far would have alerted other teams, made them even more determined to stop me. I knew, too, that those early games had been little more than a honeymoon, with the tough, physical side of Italian football still to show itself to me. So I expected it to be a lot tougher – but it was still a rude shock to find one of their players marking me from the kick-off.

37

He stuck to me like a leech throughout the whole game. He didn't even take his eyes off me to look for the ball! And if I managed to squeeze past him, there were two other defenders lying in wait for me. It was ridiculous for them really, because our other players exploited the gaps they left and we won 3–0.

To cap a disappointing day all round for me, though, I'd had to limp off ten minutes from time with that thigh injury. I could feel my legs getting heavy in the second half. Then, when I started off on a quick, sharp sprint for a ball I felt a pain in my right thigh muscle and pulled up.

I came off as a precaution really. It was probably only tiredness and stiffness and a few days' rest would cure it. Back in the dressing room, the doctor asked me what I had been eating as if that had caused the problem! But nobody seemed too concerned.

There's just a little flicker of concern crossing my mind, because Wales have a vital European Championship game with Denmark coming up in Cardiff on 9 September. And the Italian League season starts the weekend after that. They are two dates I most certainly don't want to miss. But it's only a passing fear – there's plenty of time to get fully fit for then. . . .

MONDAY 24 AUGUST: TURIN

I'm sitting in my hotel room, with my injured leg up after a day which will rank among the most traumatic of my whole life. I have to face up to the possibility of being out of football for a month or more. But I'm relieved just to be still alive, after the most terrifying flight I've ever had to suffer.

We had stayed overnight at Lecce. And my first shock came when I woke up to the screaming newspaper headlines that I was badly injured and could be out of action for six or seven weeks. Nobody had bothered to tell me, but a doctor had told reporters that I had suffered a hairline fracture of the thigh muscle.

There was a one centimetre gap in the muscle which, I gathered, could result in the muscle being badly damaged if I risked playing before it had healed. I've never suffered this kind of injury before so I'm convincing myself that the problem has been exaggerated, that I'll be back in days rather than weeks.

How did it happen? I believe it could have been caused by all the stretching we had to endure in that pre-season training, putting an extra strain and tension on muscles in a way that I have never done before. Then, in that game against Lecce I had made more five yard runs than I ever have before, trying to shake off my marker. Maybe all the stopping and starting added to the strain on the thighs.

Whatever, even the injury didn't seem to matter compared to the nightmare journey home. It was lovely and sunny when we flew out from Lecce in a private twenty-seven-seater jet hired by Juventus. And for the first hour of the journey there was nothing untoward. Then the pilot warned us to fasten our seatbelts because we were heading for some turbulent weather. . . .

The next half hour was pure terror. It was like being sat on a roller coaster 25,000 feet up as the plane lurched from side to side, climbing and then dipping, like it was tearing itself apart. I was sat towards the back, white-faced, my hands clenched together. Around me I could see the equally scared looks on the other players. One of them actually started praying.

I have flown thousands of miles in my life and been involved in a couple of nervous moments too. I was once on a plane that was struck by lightning. Then, on a journey to America, the plane suddenly fell thousands of feet before righting itself. But even they didn't compare with this.

Eventually, and thankfully, we were able to land safely, to find the streets of Turin awash with the storm. It was a hairy enough experience getting to the ground and then picking up our cars. But at least this time we were on land, at least I felt safer. It was still a relief, though, to get back to Tracey in the hotel. Then I started worrying about the injury.

For the next three days I just rested the thigh, barely walking anywhere. By the following Friday it felt fine again, I was raring to get back in action. I even thought I could play in our next game that weekend. What a shock I received when I turned up for training. 'Go back and rest it for a further week,' I was told.

MONDAY 31 AUGUST

Wales manager Mike England names me in his squad for the game against Denmark. He called me to see how the injury was progressing and I told him I was pretty certain of being fit. There were still some ten days to go and I was confident I would be able to play for Juventus the following weekend to prove my fitness.

Ironically Laudrup, who should be playing for the Danes against us, has also picked up an injury so he is doubtful too. He has an Achilles tendon problem. I reckon I've more chance of being fit than he has because I've had an extra week to rest my thigh.

FRIDAY 4 SEPTEMBER

I'm bursting to train again and play in Sunday's cup tie, but the club won't let me. They keep telling me I need more rest, but that just leaves me feeling depressed and frustrated. At Liverpool they want to get an injured player back out there on the pitch again as soon as possible. Here, maybe they treat you a little bit too much with kid gloves.

That's how I feel at this moment anyway. I know that at Anfield they would have let me try the thigh out in training to see if I was ready to come back. They always let the player have the final word. But Juventus just said no.

I'm not saying that Liverpool are right and Juventus are wrong because there's no right or wrong way in such matters. All clubs will have their different ideas. But maybe whereas at Liverpool I might have gone out feeling ninety-nine per cent fit, here you only play when you're one hundred per cent right.

SUNDAY 6 SEPTEMBER

Juventus President Giampiero Boniperti takes me to one side and tells me that I will not be allowed to play for Wales. I'm choked. Because I was so desperate to play in such a vital game I have convinced myself that I am perfectly fit.

Back in Wales, people are suggesting that Juventus have pulled a stroke on Wales, keeping me out so I will be raring to go when we start our Italian League programme at home to Como the following weekend. I'm sure that's not true. I believe Juve are an honourable club, who have the good of the player at heart with every decision they make. But I still can't help feeling a bit let-down.

When I joined the club I insisted on a clause in my contract that I would be made available for every competitive game my country played. I love playing for Wales, I love the spirit and the comradeship we have right throughout the team. I love the excitement of the build-up towards a big international game, I enjoy the celebrations if we win. Now I'm going to have to sit twiddling my thumbs, a thousand miles away.

MONDAY 7 SEPTEMBER

Wales have made a last-ditch plan to get me over for the game. Mike England has asked me to come over to Heathrow Airport, where I could be examined by an independent doctor to see if I am fit. For a moment I'm half-tempted to just pack my bags and go. But I don't take long to realize that I am a professional footballer, employed by Juventus for a lot of money.

I have signed a contract with them for three years. The last thing I need and they need is for me to cause trouble in the first month! So I go through the proper channels, ask the club if I can be examined independently. And when they veto the idea, I finally face up to the fact that I won't be going home.

What leaves me a little upset is the fact that Laudrup, who is also injured, has been given permission to join the Danish team. He will train with them and have treatment at the same time. And he will be allowed to make up his own mind on his fitness. That seems a little unfair.

But the club's president and doctor both state publically that my injury is far more serious than his. 'Ian has not yet resumed training and he will not be fit for our game with Como,' says Mr Boniperti. And our medical man, Dr Bosio, says: 'It is totally out of the question for Ian Rush to play. I have tried to explain to him but he can't understand that because he feels no pain he is not yet ready to begin kicking a ball again.'

TUESDAY 8 SEPTEMBER

Mr Boniperti and myself meet in his office to air our feelings. I feel much better in myself for having the chance to talk to him frankly – even though it has to be through an interpreter because his English is even worse than my Italian.

I have met him several times before, of course, and he has so far struck me as being a very honest man, if a little grand. We have an affinity because he used to be a team-mate of the great John Charles, the Welsh centre-forward Juventus had back in the fifties. Big John became a legend in Turin – throughout all Italy in fact – and he remains close friends with our president to this very day.

Mr Boniperti assures me that the club will never stand in the way of my country. He explains that the injury was far more serious than I had thought and that if I returned too soon I could find myself out for two or three months. But even a few days can make all the difference and I could be fit, after all, to face Como on the coming Sunday.

That cheers me up no end. I badly want to be involved on the first day of the season, if only for half a game. I'm fed up with just having to sit around like some £3.2 million club mascot! My injury has more headlines in the papers than any of the lads who have been doing the playing and it's getting me down.

WEDNESDAY 9 SEPTEMBER

I get a morning call from Mike England, who tells me that he's now almost relieved I haven't gone to play for Wales. 'If you had played and picked up an injury, the Italians would have murdered you – and me,' he said. I spoke to Welsh skipper Kevin Ratcliffe, one of my best mates, to wish the lads well that night.

But I have one big problem – how am I going to hear what's going on at Ninian Park that night while I'm so far away. I'm spending part of the time in our apartment by now and I'll be all alone this night because Tracey, thinking I'd be with Wales this week, had already made arrangements to spend a few days back in Flint with her parents.

Fortunately Ken Gorman, the reporter on the *Daily Star*, agrees to telephone me from the press box in Cardiff every twenty minutes, to keep me in touch with what's happening. I can hardly believe it when he comes on at half-time and says we're a goal up – and Andy Jones, who had stepped up from Third Division Port Vale to take my place, had helped to create it for Mark Hughes.

The next forty-five minutes seems an eternity. But then it's over, we've held that lead and I'm jumping around the apartment like someone demented. Kevin Ratcliffe rushed up to the press box as soon as he had showered – and sunk a few lagers – to tell me all about it. 'Andy was terrific and Sparky (Hughes) showed he was world-class. I'm not sure there's a place in this side for you now,' he jokes. At least I hope he was joking!

FRIDAY 11 SEPTEMBER

The longest week of my life is set to end in triumph! I've just put in a full training stint with the rest of the team and I feel great, confident that I will be fit to kick off the season against Como in two days' time. What a transformation. I didn't feel any pain from my thigh.

My parents are due to fly over tomorrow to see my first game, so I tell them to come. I pass on the same happy message to Ken Gorman, John Sadler of the *Sun* and a good mate, Gary Owen, who owns a sports shop in Queensferry. I'm feeling better now than I have for weeks. At last the agony is over . . . or so I believe.

SATURDAY 12 SEPTEMBER

The nightmare is back with me and it's worse than ever this time. For I have broken down again after just about the toughest fitness test I've ever had to face. They reckon it could be another two weeks before I'm fit.

The club's athletics coach Claudio Gaudino put me through the test – a tortuous series of twisting and stretching exercises that I couldn't help thinking would have been more suited to a ballerina than a footballer. At the end I'm knackered. I'm worried that all the stress might have aggravated the injury. All I can do is rest it for a few days and hope it will clear up the pain I'm feeling right now.

I still had to travel with the team to our pre-match head-quarters at Villa Perosa. But I felt the loneliest man in the world, knowing that I was out the next day. So, after dinner, I asked if I could go back to my apartment to see my mum and dad who were due to arrive that night. It might be against the rules, but they did let me leave.

I was choked when I went back to the flat to see my folks. They had never even been in an aeroplane before. As it happened, though, they thoroughly enjoyed the experience and they were thrilled just to be over in Turin to see me.

SUNDAY 13 SEPTEMBER

I mightn't have been playing that afternoon, but I was still the hero to the thousands of Juventus fans who were crammed outside the stadium when I arrived. I was besieged by them as I tried to make my way from my car to the players' entrance. The police tried to form a passage for me, but that didn't stop those frenzied supporters from getting at me.

By now, I've started to become accustomed to the Italian way of footballing life. I've had people come up to me in the street and touch me, just to make sure I'm real! But I wasn't ready for the antics of one supporter, who grabbed me round the neck and planted a huge kiss on my mouth. What made it really embarrassing was the fact that it was a man! For a split second I felt my blood boil and I was ready to belt him one. But then, luckily, I saw the funny side of it all and all I did was laugh. People sure are different over here. . . .

The game itself was a bit of an anti-climax after all the hysterical build-up to the season in the local press. With half the team made up of new faces we obviously took time to settle into any real rhythm. But at least we beat Como 1–0 with a penalty near the end. And to win without playing that well was a sign that things ought to get much better when we're more at home with each other.

We had a EUFA Cup tie the following midweek in Malta. I went over with the team even though the manager had told me I wouldn't be risked because the game was not important enough. I actually trained well over there, my thigh feeling much stronger again after forty-eight hours' rest.

I was a bit of a celebrity in Malta because hundreds of them seemed to be Liverpool supporters. They wanted to know everything about Anfield – more than they did about Juventus. Mind, the side showed the Maltese that we could play a bit too, winning 4–0. So the season hadn't begun too badly. But I was burning to become a part of it and made up my mind I would play the following weekend, come hell or high water.

· FOUR ·

Hot and Cold

FRIDAY 18 SEPTEMBER

The manager Rino Marchesi is not very happy, but I am
adamant – I'm playing in our next game at Empoli on
Sunday. I've been out a month through the thigh injury and
still the boss says I need another week's rest. But I have
trained normally this morning with the rest of the team and
now I just want to get on with the job I was brought over
here to do.

In the end he relents and says I can play, at least for half
a game. That's music to my ears. So I'm wearing the biggest
smile for weeks as I go home to Tracy at our apartment.
We've moved in fully now, but we're still desperately short
of furniture. We've got some coming over from North Wales
and we've been scouring the shops in Turin searching for
the rest.

Tracy is thrilled for me ... and more than a little relieved!
She's had to bear the brunt of my misery these past few
weeks. I have to remember it's been a tough time for her too.
In fact, we've both been trying to do so much it's a wonder
we can keep awake. She's up at 6.30 every week morning to

47

go to an adult class at school to learn Italian. I get up around seven to drive her there. Those who know me know that the early morning is not exactly my peak time!

Then we spend the afternoons organizing the buying and delivery of the furniture, on top of a language lesson at home twice a week. It's also surprising how many little jobs there are to organize. For example, I've spent weeks waiting for the car the club promised me. I don't like going to them complaining all the time, but there isn't much alternative.

We've only been married just over three months and it's difficult enough to adjust to that change in your lifestyle, let alone the problems of moving to a foreign land. It's funny, I can remember Ronnie Moran, the coach at Liverpool, saying when Ronnie Whelan got married: 'Well, that's him knackered for six months. . . .'

It was said partly as a joke, but now I know what he meant. Don't get me wrong, I think marriage is wonderful and I really couldn't imagine life without Tracy. It's just that you do have extra responsibilities to face up to and it takes time to get used to it all.

SUNDAY 20 SEPTEMBER

Empoli is just a small township in Tuscany, midway between Florence and Pisa. Just a dot on the map to most people but a place that will always remain on my mind. For it gave me a jolting, frustrating first taste of what football in the Italian First Division is to be about this season. It's not total gloom – at least I've come through my first game since injury; what a relief! But there was still disappointment when I trudged off the pitch after we'd lost 1–0.

We'd made the two-and-a-half-hour coach journey down from Turin the day before and I was really getting excited at the match ahead. I'd done pretty well in pre-season games, but this at last was the real thing. I wasn't nervous at all, I just wanted to pull on that Juventus strip, get on the pitch and get on with the game.

I roomed, as usual, with Laudrup the night before the game. We didn't talk much at all. He's a quiet lad who just wants to live his own life. The manager had us both together before the kick-off, to tell us exactly how he wanted us to play, what he expected from us.

What I hadn't bargained for was the heat! It was 110 degrees out in the middle of the packed little stadium, which held only about 20,000 people. Empoli were everybody's favourites for relegation – they had had five points deducted for some infringement even before a ball was kicked. And really they shouldn't live with giants like Juventus – it's a bit like Walsall or Notts County trying to compete with teams like Liverpool or Manchester United.

The sweat was pouring off me within minutes of the kick-off. And it wasn't only the heat which was making my temperature rise. The first time I went to make a run I was halted by a defender pulling my shirt. And that set the tempo for the game. I had to struggle to keep my temper as defenders obstructed me in every way they could.

And what was making it all worse was that the referee just accepted it all. He didn't even pull the offenders up, when he should have stamped on it from the start by booking the first culprit. A yellow card in the first five minutes might have had the desired effect of preventing the others indulging in their petty fouls.

If my shirt wasn't being pulled, there'd be a defender's arms wrapped around me or a body in the way preventing me from making any kind of run. It was sickening. I had to fight to control my temper, to make sure I didn't commit the cardinal sin of retaliating.

The only goal came from Empoli's Swedish striker Johnny

Ekstrom ten minutes into the second half. They battled hard, we just didn't start playing so we didn't deserve any other result. But what's troubling me as much as anything on the journey back home is the fact that I didn't receive a single chance in the whole game.

I could have put up with all the aggro from the other side, laughed at it, if I felt we looked a side who would create a lot of chances. But we just never looked like scoring. One newspaper reporter, who wrote an article on my performance specifically, revealed that I touched the ball just a dozen times! At Liverpool I've run around a lot less and had twice as much of the ball.

MONDAY 21 SEPTEMBER

You would think that Juventus had just been relegated, the way the papers have slaughtered us this morning. 'A terrible disaster' was the screaming headline across one front page. What will it be like if things get really rough?

I also read that the manager is criticizing my performance, saying I will have to work harder, to go looking for the ball more. Well, if that's what he wants, I'll do it. But Juventus knew what kind of player I was when they signed me. I'm not a George Best, who can take on a whole defence with one mazy dribble.

I need players around me, especially in midfield, who can give the ball in the penalty area. Then my job is to make the chances count. I feel that some straight talking is needed, so I spoke to Mr Marchesi, who denied making any criticism of me. He is a quiet, gentle sort of person and I believe him. I know also that he must be under pressure of his own, losing even a match is a crime to our newspapermen.

I must say here that the supporters are totally different. They were great. Those who did stop me in the street had only words of encouragement to give me. Playing down in the south of Italy, for Roma or Napoli, you can't even walk the street in safety if you're a footballer because you'd be mobbed by hordes of fans. Right now, I'm grateful that most of our fans leave me to walk in peace.

SUNDAY 27 SEPTEMBER

There are 45,000 fans jostled into the Stadio Comunale to watch us play Pescara and I know a lot of them have come to see my home debut. And those supporters, bless them, give me a rousing welcome as the teams walk out through the canvas tunnel and onto the pitch.

The pre-match warm up here is different to England inasmuch as it's done behind closed doors, in the gym near our dressing room. I don't do much, just a couple of stretching exercises to loosen the muscles. So it's straight into action when we come out, on a beautiful autumn afternoon with the temperature touching the eighties. Mind, after Empoli's furnace, it seems almost cool, and so is our display for the first forty-three minutes – you can sense a lot of nerves and jitters among the players. We need a goal to settle us down. And then, with half-time approaching, comes the magic moment.

Laudrup makes a good break down the right, but his cross is not a very good one. Their sweeper is at the near post to chest it down. But I read the situation, nip in front of him as the ball comes down from his chest and, before he could get his boot to it, I whack it as hard as I can. It's an instinctive thing, you have a vague idea of where the goal is and you just hit it in the general direction, hoping it will be on target. This one was ... perfectly.

The crowd explode. The firecrackers sound like a machine gun being let off in the Curva Filadelfia – the ground's equivalent to Anfield's Kop – where our most vociferous supporters congregate. My team-mates are mobbing me, a mixture of relief and joy showing on their faces. And I feel like a king.

It is a fabulous feeling, much more satisfying than my first goal for Liverpool even. That came in a European Cup tie against a Finnish team called Oulu. We were about five goals up already that night when I came on as sub and scored a simple tap-in. There was some satisfaction in that but not a lot of feeling of achievement.

But this was special because I don't feel I've been under so much pressure to score in my whole life. I suppose there was a fair bit of pressure on me when I moved from Chester to Liverpool for £350,000 and became Britain's costliest teenager. I reckon I was too young and green then, though, to feel it all.

I reckoned in the years following that I had learned all about living with pressure at Liverpool. But it was nothing like the intensity I had been forced to endure since I came to Italy. I came with one simple objective – to try my best, to find out for myself if I could succeed in a League that boasts the world's greatest players. As far as I'm concerned, what I cost and what I earn has nothing to do with it. I can only try my best.

But you try telling that to the Italian press! They don't merely expect to see Superman out there in Juve's number nine shirt, they demand it. They are the worst in the world for building you up and knocking you down. One day they'd have you ready for suicide, the next you'd be as high as a kite if you believe what they write about you. It's easy to say that the only answer is to shrug it off. Even footballers are only human, we have feelings like everyone else.

Back to the match, and the crowd are still celebrating and chanting my name as we walk off at half-time. The dressing room is bubbling now, it's amazing what difference a goal can make. And we're really on song in the second half.

It's only a matter of time before we score again. And on the hour it comes. I pick up a long ball played downfield, turn inside a defender and then find only the goalkeeper blocking my path. In the past I would have taken the ball up to him then tried to slot it round him or chipped it over him as he advanced.

But this time the keeper didn't really advance. And that left me a bit flummoxed. I dummied him one way, then the other until I got past him. By then, though, there were a couple of defenders back on the line. So I just blasted it from about fifteen yards. I was falling as I hit it but I saw the ball swerve spectacularly into the top corner.

It looked a sensational goal, but maybe I could have made it look a lot easier. I'm not one for blasting shots, stroking the ball into the net is more my game. Blasting you'll get maybe four out of ten, my way you look for eight out of ten. Yet the crowd thought it was a wonderful goal. In Italy they thrive on the spectacular, the theatrical.

Anyway, we carried on playing some really good football. I missed a chance for a hat trick before Favero, our full back, scored our third. With twenty minutes still left, we should have scored five. But we started getting cocky and arrogant, everyone wanting to do clever things on the ball instead of keeping it simple.

They pulled one back with a quarter of an hour to go and all of a sudden we were struggling. They almost got a second, when a shot hit the post. Goodness knows what would have happened if they had. Still, the fans were still chanting and singing an hour after the match when I left for home.

Tracy had gone back with Laudrup's girlfriend, so I went home with my best pal at the club, Pasquale Bruno. We live quite close up in the hills and we've become really good mates. He only joined the club in the summer, from Como, so we've been new boys together. And he's been great, going out of his way to make me feel at home.

He's a rough, tough defender on the pitch – I wouldn't fancy having him mark me every week. But off it he's as daft as I am, so we have a lot of laughs together. Except when he's driving. I reckon I'm quite a fast operator on the roads but he's just plain crazy!

I've got a few other particularly good pals at the club. Sergio Brio has taken the time and trouble to get me involved in things, while our goalkeeper Stefano Tacconi is a real extrovert, who has the whole dressing room laughing with his antics. He reminds me of Bruce Grobbelaar – I reckon the old saying that all keepers are lunatics is not so far from the truth.

Mind, Tacconi is one of those guys who can't keep his mouth shut, even when the Italian press are around. Whenever they want to raise a bit of a scandal story they go to him, ask him some loaded questions and he can't help answering them. He gets fined by the club from time to time for the outrageous things he's supposed to have said in print.

I'm not too sure what the feelings of the other players are towards me, though. We don't seem to communicate much at all. It's not the most comfortable dressing room I've known, I guess I was spoiled by all the fun I enjoyed at Anfield. Here there's a kind of tension in the air, something I've never known before.

And I can't help but get the feeling that I'm very much on trial, that the Italian players – all bar a few of them – are wary of me. It doesn't exactly help towards the process of settling down with a new club, in a new country.

I know that if the roles were reversed, if this had been Liverpool and we had signed a new foreign player, I would have gone out of my way to make him feel at home, take him out and show him around. But this is a land where things are so different. Maybe it will just take time; that they want to be 110 per cent sure about you before they make any moves.

WEDNESDAY 30 SEPTEMBER

My first taste of European action with my new club, but it's all very much an anticlimax as we beat the Maltese part-timers 3–0 in the second leg of our UEFA Cup tie. I get a goal, five minutes from the end, and it's a bit of a collector's item as it comes from my head. I don't get too many of those. The main object of the exercise, though, was to get me that bit closer to full fitness. I still felt I was that yard short of my normal pace following my long lay off.

Such was the lack of interest in the game that we kicked off at five o'clock, when the streets of Turin are choked with the traffic jams of workers going home. We had just about 15,000 at the stadium to watch us. Afterwards Tracy and I went to spend the evening at Michael Laudrup's home.

His Danish team-mate Klaus Berggreen was also there. The crucial European Championship game between Denmark and Wales was only two weeks away, but we never mentioned it. Instead, Berggreen kept us entertained with his jokes and his humour – like all Danes, he speaks perfect English.

He was a smashing bloke, full of life and vitality, just like the popular image we have of the Danes, Laudrup is such a different personality. He is quiet, almost withdrawn. But he is a few years younger than me, so perhaps he is still a bit shy.

SUNDAY 4 OCTOBER

If our defeat at Empoli two weeks ago left me disappointed, today I'm close to despair. We've just lost 2–1 at Verona and I hardly had a kick. The service from our midfield was virtually non-existent. I'm not one to make excuses for myself – I'll say straightaway if I've had a bad game, if I've not done my job. What's grieving me about this game, though, is that I never had the chance to do my job.

I wanted to help, I ran around as much as I could trying to create openings for myself. But the ball just didn't reach me. It's all so frustrating . . . I only hope that it's not going to be like this all the way through the season. But we do have a lot of new faces in the team and it's only our fourth league game. Perhaps things will improve as the season goes on. I desperately hope so!

After the game Bruno and I leave the rest of the team to go and meet our wives who are in nearby Venice. We spent the whole of the next day just exploring this city on water – and were enchanted by what we saw. I've been to a great many places in this world, but this really was one of the most breathtaking places I had ever visited.

We did all the usual tourist things, enjoying a ride on the famous gondolas, having a go on the speedboats. It was an amazing sight, people's front windows perched just a few feet above the water. Even traffic lights were hoisted above the waterways to keep the various craft flowing. We loved it all so much that we make a pledge to visit Venice again in the new year.

SUNDAY 11 OCTOBER

Come to Italy for the sunshine, they told me a few months ago. You could have fooled me! We've just beaten Roma, the early season pacesetters at the top of the league, 1–0 at home. But I feel more like someone who has just endured a game of water polo than football. It was like trying to play football in the Mersey!

The weather had been atrocious for two days before the game, with heavy rain turning the pitch into a quagmire when we kicked off. But if we thought that was tough, the second half was unbelievable. It was played in a torrential downpour which produced huge puddles all over the playing surface. It was impossible to hack the ball more than a couple of yards, even when you gave it a full-blooded wallop.

I think the referee only allowed the game to finish because there had already been a goal scored, by our skipper Cabrini just three minutes before the interval. Mind, big Tacconi was our real hero – he saved a penalty ten minutes before we went in front.

At the end I was absolutely shattered. Running about in those conditions leaves your legs feeling like jelly. But I was relieved as well. At least I hadn't been injured, which meant I was fit and well to join up with the Welsh squad for our game in Copenhagen in three days' time.

MONDAY 12 OCTOBER

I have to fly from Milan to Copenhagen at noon, so the club taxi picks me up at home at 9.30 for the ninety-minutes drive. Don't think I'm lording it ... I have to pay the fare out of my wages! I get there to find Laudrup already booked in, along with his Danish colleague Preben Elkjaer, who plays for Verona.

We all boarded the same plane, but we couldn't sit together. They were travelling business class, while I was scrunched up at the back in economy class. You'll never start kidding yourself you're a superstar when you travel with

Wales! Still, the flight took less than two hours so I laughed it off.

But there were a couple of Italian journalists flying over to Denmark with us. I should have known they'd make a meal of it. The story was all over the papers in Italy by the evening ... 'Rush is a second class citizen'. By now I just laugh at all the stories that appear in the papers.

The rest of the Welsh party had arrived from London a couple of hours before me, but they waited for me to join them before shaking off the effects of the flight with a training session. It was great to see all the lads again. I have been a little bit lonely in Italy because of the language barrier. Now I don't seem to be able to stop talking.

I take a fair bit of stick from the others when we train – Was that an Italian shot? Is that an Italian exercise? Is that an Italian haircut? – the usual kind of mickey-taking. But I lap it up. I love the sense of humour among the players in the Welsh squad and at Liverpool. In Italy things seem a lot more serious. When I first joined Juventus I was wary of every instruction I was told by anyone.

If someone said go to a particular room for your kit, or there's a telephone call or whatever I wouldn't believe them at first. I'd just stand there and look dumb. They must have thought I was an idiot! There's no joking in Italy.

WEDNESDAY 14 OCTOBER

Despite playing pretty well and deserving a draw, Wales have lost 1–0 to Denmark, so our battle to win a place in the European Championship finals will have to go right to the bitter end.

If we had beaten the Danes we would have booked our passage to West Germany next summer. Now we have to beat Czechoslovakia in Prague next month. If we don't, the

Danes will go through. So it's all up to us. But because there is still so much to play for the atmosphere among the players is far from despondent.

I was disappointed with my own performance. I had been drained of energy in that game against Roma just three days earlier and I just didn't feel as sharp as I would have hoped. I missed one chance in the first half when Mark Hughes made the opening and my first touch let me down.

Mark was playing only his second game of the season, but he did well. However, we both had to put up with some unmerciful stick the Danish defenders were handing out. We had lumps kicked out of us ... my ankle is sore and swollen.

The Danes had complained bitterly, and publically, about the alleged caveman tactics of the Welsh players after we had beaten them in Cardiff a month earlier. It was all calculated to influence the officials in charge of our game now and I reckon it worked. We got next to nothing from the referee while their players were rolling over theatrically every time they were tackled – and winning free kicks.

THURSDAY 15 OCTOBER

Now I'm really back among my own folk! Mark Hughes and I are sat with Kevin Ratcliffe in the corner of a bar in Chester, savouring British beer again – and just loving listening to the babble of noise around us, in a language we can both understand.

Because Italy have an international match the following Sunday all First Division games are postponed, which means I have been able to come home for a few days break. All the northern based lads in the Welsh squad flew up from Heathrow to Manchester and a few of us decided we had earned a drink or two. The others have left now, so it's only Mark and myself.

And it's doing the pair of us good to talk about the problems we have faced in foreign countries. If I've been feeling a trifle sorry for myself, I only have to think what Sparky has endured this last twelve months to make me realize that my time in Italy has been a cakewalk by comparison.

At least I've had my football to keep me going at Juventus. That concentrates your mind. But since Terry Venables dropped Mark from his team at Barcelona he has had to live through a nightmare. That game for Wales the day before was only his second competitive game of the season – and both were for the Welsh.

He's been laughing and joking with the lads for the past few days, but I could sense that deep down he was still shell-shocked by the awful way Barcelona have treated him. He's been forced to kick his heels for most of the year, because the Spanish club have no reserve team.

Now I know that a lot of folk won't have any sympathy with a player who is earning more in a week than they will in a couple of months. And if he's picking up the cash for nothing, well lucky him! But life is not all about money, all about a thriving bank balance. If you're getting nothing out of your job, no satisfaction, you're an unhappy man.

What's worse for Mark is that his club will not give him a second chance. I can sense that he's grown up a lot in the past twelve months. His form on the field was good, apart from the natural bit of rust that will be there when you go so long between games. All he needs is to be playing regularly.

And he needs a gesture of faith by his club. Surely that's not too much to ask, after all, they did shell out £2 million on him, so they must believe he's got something to offer.

SATURDAY 17 OCTOBER

It's nice to know I haven't been forgotten! The Kop at Anfield gave me a rousing cheer as I took my seat in the directors box – I guess you have to slum it sometimes! – to watch Liverpool beat QPR 4–0 and maintain their amazing unbeaten start to the season.

It was a strange game. Rangers had a couple of real chances to take the lead before the lads got into full swing. Then some of their play was delightful, with Beardsley and Barnes, the new boys up front, both contributing some lovely touches.

I'm delighted that things are going so well for Liverpool. Yet not even for one moment did any feeling of regret that I was no longer part of it all come over me. Everybody was really nice to Tracy and myself – she came along because we were flying from Manchester to London and back to Turin directly after the game – yet it was a bit of a weird feeling, not being part of it any more.

I had gone to the ground the day before, to join the lads in training and to get some treatment to my ankle, which was still sore after the buffeting by the Danes. Kenny Dalglish, the manager, remains a good friend and he has always told me I was welcome back at Anfield any time I was in the area.

Of course, I can't be back for a single day without landing myself in some trouble. I have a good contract with Nike Sportswear – I happen to think their gear is great anyway, so to get paid for wearing it is a bonus. But I just picked up an old track-suit top from the players' kit to go training and emblazoned across it is the name of a rival sports goods company! When a local photographer snapped my picture – which appeared in the newspapers the next morning – I wasn't the most popular guy around. . . .

Still, I had a long chat with Kenny in his office about my

hopes and my fears in Italy. I speak to him on the telephone quite regularly. He has told me that if I ever needed advice from an older head, he would be only too pleased to help. And I've taken him up on it.

He's even sent me tapes of Liverpool's games and a magnificent ninety-minutes video on *The History of Liverpool*. That will help to keep me warm on those cold winter nights!

Graeme Souness, my former captain at Liverpool and now manager of Glasgow Rangers, is another friend with whom I speak regularly on the phone. Graeme played in Italy for a couple of years, so he knows all the problems. He's also a very shrewd guy, so he knows most of the answers, too!

I called him early in my time in Italy to ask his advice about a particular matter. And what he said was spot on. Now we communicate quite often. It's great to have people like Kenny and Graeme to fall back on. They both have a wealth of experience. And being successful managers, they know how to bring the best out of other people.

I reckon that, judging by the start of Juventus's season in Italy, those phone lines are going to be kept pretty busy during the months ahead. . . .

· FIVE ·

Prague Winter

WEDNESDAY 21 OCTOBER

The day after my twenty-sixth birthday. And I ruefully recall
that old saying: 'Beware of Greeks bearing gifts'. Especially
when these 'gifts' are in the form of the battering I've just
been given in Athens, where we've just lost 1–0 to the hatchet
men of Panathinaikos in the first leg of our UEFA Cup tie.

To say it was rough would be like saying that Everest is a
pretty big hill! It was murder, the tactics of the Greek
defenders made those back home in Italy seem like choirboys.
And what made it all the worse was the fact that the referee,
who had given me no protection at all, was Mr Ron Bridges
from North Wales!

When I first heard he was in charge I was delighted. The
other players asked me about him and I told them he was
top class. I think that in the main British referees are the
best in Europe. And I was all the more pleased to have one
for this tie, because the Greeks are notorious for the ferocity
of their tackling, especially before their own fanatical supporters.

I had met Bridges a couple of times at presentations back

in North Wales, but I wouldn't claim to say I know him. We'd never even had a drink together. But the Italian papers, as only they can, suddenly carried stories that he was a personal friend of mine. And the reports, naturally, found their way into Greek papers as well.

That really fuelled up the Greeks. Ironically, Bridges had refereed Liverpool's game the previous weekend, so when I arrived in Athens their reporters were asking me if I had taken him out to dinner afterwards! I hadn't even spoken to him, but it made no difference to the stories that appeared on the morning of the match. I have no way of knowing whether or not the pressure on the referee got to him, but in my opinion, he did not have a good game.

The game had been going for just two minutes when I was kicked, quite deliberately and cold-bloodedly, on my injured ankle. I felt that the defender should have been booked straight away. But he was let off scot-free.

I had to go off for five minutes to have treatment on the ankle. And I was still off the field when they scored the only goal – a cracking twenty-five yard drive. I limped back on, to get whacked again right on the same ankle by the same defender. Once again, no action was taken.

I suppose that if Bridges had cautioned the player doing all the kicking the crowd would have gone berserk, claiming the match was fixed. As it was, we were given nothing. Twice our players went down inside their penalty area and play was waved on. I was kicked five times altogether on that same ankle. And we had a brilliant goal direct from a free kick chalked off because we had a player caught offside. The referee clearly took the view that our man was interfering with play, even though he was nowhere near the flight of the ball and, in my experience, many referees would have allowed the goal to stand.

I took a lot of flak from my team-mates at the end, 'If he's a good referee, what are the bad ones like back in Britain?' they said. I didn't speak to Bridges either before or after the game. What I do know is that I never want a local referee in charge of a game I play in again.

I thought he was one of the top referees in Europe but after this I've changed my mind. Now I think he's just average. With the benefit of hindsight, he was clearly on a hiding to nothing. I felt that I did not get sufficient protection, but if he had come down hard on defenders, he would have been open to criticism from the Greek players and press who would have claimed that he was biased against them. It would clearly have been better, because of all the pre-match hype, if he had not been selected to referee the match.

SUNDAY 25 OCTOBER

Our depressing away record continues. We have just lost 2–1 to Inter Milan at the San Siro Stadium, in a poor game in which neither side played well. We came back from a goal down to draw level through Di Agostini and looked as if we might win it for a while.

But they got the winner late on. What worries me, though, is that once more we've barely created a chance. I did have one which I tried to tuck away in the way I did at Liverpool, but it did not come off. I was some way from full fitness – my ankle was still swollen and had to be heavily strapped.

But it's still the fourth game in which I have failed to score and I took a bit of stick from Inter's fans. 'Blissett, Blissett!' they chanted at me. They were comparing me with poor Luther Blissett, who spent the worst year of his career at AC Milan a few years ago.

MONDAY 26 OCTOBER

Another battering in the press, the most hysterical it's been yet. Some of the reporters have written me off already as nowhere good enough and nowhere near worth the money the club paid for me. I know I have to accept my share of responsibility for what has been a disappointing start to the season.

But I still tell the reporters who jostle around me – please wait until the end of the season until you make your judgement on me. And, bless him, Tacconi dives in fearlessly on my behalf. He strides up to the pressmen and blasts them.

'Leave Rush alone,' he roars. 'Remember that Platini took five months to adjust to Italian football. So why do you expect Ian to have mastered it in five weeks? You are cruel and unfair to him. Give him time.' I don't know if it will have any effect on the journalists, but it's great to have a colleague sticking up for me. He's right, too. Platini was just about the best player in the world – or vying with Maradona for the title – during his spell here. If he needed virtually a full season to adjust, surely I'll need that, and more.

SUNDAY I NOVEMBER

I badly needed some kind of inspiration to get the press off my back and it's come today – we've beaten Avelino 3–0 and I've scored. Now, suddenly, the multi-lire flop of a week ago is a hero again!

As I have stated before, you can't take too much notice of the newspapers, no matter whether they are worshipping you as a genius or claiming you're ready for the knacker's yard. But it will be nice to have some cheerful headlines in the morning for a change.

Stories have begun to circulate that I'm really at odds with my team-mates now. That I don't speak to any of them and that there is a hate campaign building up among several of them towards me. It's not as bad as that, but I have to confess that things aren't exactly what I'd hoped.

I still sense this unease in our changing room all the time. It's not something you can put your finger on, just an atmosphere. I wonder whether some of them resent the way our supporters seem to have taken to me. And the fact that when I joined Juventus my Italian was strictly limited didn't help, either.

By now, though, I really am working hard to master the language. And I am improving – honest! Perhaps when I can really hold a conversation in Italian things will improve. I thought I'd scored the first goal today, but it was given as an own goal. Just my luck! I did score the second fifteen minutes from time when I saw a half gap and blasted a shot home. At least the players showed their delight at my goal, which was encouraging.

WEDNESDAY 4 NOVEMBER

Disaster. We are out of Europe, despite beating Panathinaikos 3–2. It put the aggregate level at 3–3, but the Greeks go through on the away goals rule. And I'm totally sickened. We had just struck a bit of good form the previous weekend and were supremely confident of getting through to the third round of the UEFA Cup.

Maybe we were just a little too confident. But we were always fighting a losing battle after the Greeks led 1–0 and then 2–1. And although we had eleven minutes to sneak the tie after leading 3–2, we just couldn't make all our pressure count.

To be booted out of European combat, especially by a team we ought to have buried, is tough on our supporters, who made their feelings pretty clear with their whistling and jeering as we left the pitch. And the dressing room was like a morgue. I've never felt particularly happy in there, but right now it's worse than ever.

SUNDAY 8 NOVEMBER

At least Juventus have shown some character today. We've shaken off the nightmare defeat in Europe to pull off our first away win of the season, 2–1 in Pisa. And we deserved it. It was a tough, uncompromising game and we outplayed them.

I came up against an English centre half for the first and probably only time in Italy, Paul Elliott. I'd played against Paul before, in his days with Luton and Aston Villa, and had the odd pint in the player's lounge with him afterwards, so I knew him slightly.

But I wasn't too sure what I thought of him when our winning goal which I turned over the line from a yard out was credited as an own goal by him! The ball had struck him and was probably going over the line anyway, but I was there to make sure. At Liverpool, there would have been no question about it – my goal.

In Italy, though, they base so much on the evidence of television. So, when the name of the goalscorer came into doubt, I said to the rest of the players: 'You just watch the goal on TV then you'll see who scored.' What I had forgotten is that there was a technicians' strike in Italy that weekend and none of the games were filmed! I know that the main thing in football is to win and it doesn't really matter who scores the goals. But over here so much emphasis and import-ance is attached to the number of goals after your name I could have done with this one.

Still, we had collected two more points and I had come through unscathed for the crucial Wales game in Czechoslovakia in three days time. So I was more than happy as I flew back from Pisa and, yes, I did get a glimpse of the famous tower and it really is incredible.

Paul Elliott flew back to London with me. We had another spare weekend coming up because of another Italian international game, so he was going home to visit his folks. We had a long chat about the ups and downs of life in Italy. Like me, his major concern was over the language problem.

It was late at night when I arrived at the Welsh team's headquarters in one of the hotels dotted around Heathrow Airport. But Mike England, the Welsh manager, was waiting there to see me, just to make sure there were no problems with injury or the like.

'Thank God you're fine. That means that all the lads are here safely, although there are one or two of them carrying niggling knocks,' said Mike.

What had happened to the Welsh before one of the most vital games in their history was nothing short of a scandal. The Football Association had allowed all the players in England's squad to have the weekend off, with their equally important game in Yugoslavia also being staged on the coming Wednesday. But they refused point-blank to grant the same privilege to Welsh players in the Football League.

It was a decision which stinks and one which speaks volumes for the totally selfish and arrogant attitudes of those in high office at the FA. It was those same people who had brought poverty to Wales and Northern Ireland by deciding that the British Championship should be scrapped.

That annual competition was the lifeblood to the Welsh and the Irish, it brought in the revenue that kept the Associations going and helped to foster the game in both countries. As a Welshman, and proud of it, I find the smug 'I'm all right Jack' outlook of some Englishmen nauseating.

Poor Mike England had been forced to sweat right through

the weekend, not knowing who would be fit, not knowing what kind of team he would be able to field. I realize that Mark Hughes, who had just moved on loan to Bayern Munich and was by all accounts playing brilliantly in the West German Bundesliga, and myself would have had to have played on this weekend anyway.

But at least Wales would have had nine out of their eleven players fully rested and free from the knocks and bruises you pick up in every game. It's not asking for the moon just to be treated on a par with the English. After all, the League would be much poorer without the Welsh, Scottish and Irish players who help to make it up.

WEDNESDAY 11 NOVEMBER

This has to be the rock bottom day of the season, one of the worst days of my whole life in fact. We are out of the European Championships, having been beaten 2–0 by a Czech team we should have murdered. And I missed chances that would have earned us a resounding victory.

The stadium in Prague was eerily quiet, almost like a tomb, with only about 6,000 fans turning up to watch the game. And for the opening half hour we threatened to bury their team in it. We played some of the best, most constructive and methodical football I have ever seen any Welsh team play.

We were so much on top that their players were running in circles trying to stop us. And when they did get the ball they were so lacking in confidence they could do nothing to break our stranglehold. Yet three times in that spell I came tantalizingly close to getting a goal which, I am convinced, would have set us up for a sensational win.

I hit one drive on the volley, seeing it fly a couple of feet high. Then I actually scrambled the ball past their goalkeeper, only to see it cleared off the line by a defender.

Then I got in a header which flashed just the wrong side of the bar. Then I beat the keeper to a ball at the near post, only to see it deflect to safety off that post. It was sickening and it left me feeling nervous.

When a team is that much on top, they have to turn their advantage into a tangible lead. Otherwise football has a habit of kicking you in the teeth. And so it proved this night. Their first attack of any kind was helped by a couple of defensive slips, and one of their strikers let fly with a thunderbolt from thirty yards which left Neville Southall groping.

It was a brilliant strike, an inspirational goal. But, if your luck is not in, it is the kind of shot which would have ended high in the crowd. To give our lads credit, no heads went down. We gave everything, and then a bit more, to get back on terms and then snatch the victory we needed.

But for all the frantic scrambles in the Czech goalmouth, for all the half-chances that came up, we just couldn't do it. They scored a second from a free kick right at the death. And there were tears in the eyes of our players as we trudged off the field. Another golden chance for Wales to reach the finals of a major competition had disappeared.

We knew that the result would leave the job of our manager hanging by a thread. Poor Mike had come heartbreakingly close to leading Wales to the last two World Cup finals and the previous European Championship finals and I'd suffered with him all the way. Now this latest chapter of anguish was too much to bear. We knew there would be calls for his head from some quarters.

Yet Mike and his assistant Doug Livermore had done everything right in our whole build-up to the game. No team could have been better prepared, if it had been managed by Brian Clough, Bob Paisley or anyone. We blew it for him out there on the pitch. And I must take the major portion of the blame.

'If anyone deserves the axe after that, it should be me,' I told the pressmen who had travelled to Prague. 'I had the chances and I missed them. Mike England did everything he possibly could. He deserves to be applauded rather than suffer any criticism for this.'

If the mood of the players in the changing room was one of dark despair, it changed to outright anger when Leighton James, once a great Welsh player himself and covering the match for a radio station, stormed in to tell us that we had just been verbally blasted by Alun Evans, the secretary of the Welsh FA.

'I was so angry with him, I just had to tell you,' he blurted. And that left us furious, especially when we heard that the manager's job was already the subject of discussion by various Welsh FA members. We were told there was to be a meeting to decide Mike's future and we exploded with rage.

There were amazing scenes at the airport in Prague. We were flying straight back to London after the game, when the players held their own meeting on the tarmac. All the senior players, men like skipper Kevin Ratcliffe, Peter Nicholas, Neville Southall and myself, huddled together and made a decision which could have shocked the whole footballing world.

If Mike England was sacked, then we would go on strike. We would refuse to play for our country again. It all might smack of anarchy and mob rule in the cold light of day. But as we examined the situation our emotions were running dangerously high. We were so bitter and angered by the way the manager was being blamed we were ready to do anything.

It was after midnight when we arrived back at Heathrow and to our hotel. Most of the players stayed overnight and we sat for hours just discussing the rights and wrongs of the situation. Footballers are resilient people – you have to be in a profession which can so often hit you below the belt –

you've got to learn to be able to bounce back from any adversity.

So gradually the mood did lift slightly, a few jokes were cracked. But while your face might smile, you're still hurting inside. The laughter was pretty hollow, believe me. But at least it was better than sitting alone in your room.

Some time in the early hours, we were joined by Terry Butcher and Chris Woods, two of the England party who had also flown back to Heathrow after their remarkable 4–1 win in Yugoslavia. That had put them through to the finals, so they were obviously both in high spirits.

But they were both good blokes. I met them in Israel back in June when Rangers were over there with Liverpool for friendly matches and they didn't rub it in by talking about their summer in West Germany. They sensed the depressed mood among those of our lads who were still awake. So there was a lot of small talk, but not much football mentioned at all.

· SIX ·

Maradona Magic

You sometimes get the feeling in life that you just can't win no matter what you do. We've just beaten Cesena 1–0, which would have been our fifth league win in a row. But to look round the dressing room, you'd think we'd just been tanked with everyone so low.

We might as well have been beaten, because we all know deep down that we are going to lose the two points because of a firecracker thrown by one of our fans at half time. It was just one of a score of fireworks tossed down in celebration rather than mischief.

It happens every game, home and away, they explode but they're really harmless most of the time. Unfortunately this particular one struck one of the Cesena players and hurt him enough as he had to be taken to hospital. It was a freak accident as the firework was thrown from at least forty yards away and could just as easily have hit one of our players.

But the rulers of Italian football have recently been stamping down hard on terrace troubles. Napoli had just been awarded the points despite losing 1–0 at Pisa because one of

74

their players had been hit by a coin. So we expected the same fate and our fears were confirmed a few days later.

While I'm on the side of those trying to stamp out the worldwide problem of violence by the so-called supporters, I still feel the punishment inflicted on us far outweighed the crime. At the worst I feel that the game should be replayed, behind closed doors if necessary.

Anyway, it was a hell of a way to end a week which had seen Wales knocked out of the European Championships. The Italians had also had their fair share of aggro, mind, with Cabrini announcing he was retiring from international football because he could no longer be guaranteed a place in their national team.

I can understand his attitude in wanting to leave the world stage at the top. He had captained Italy, played in the team which won the World Cup in 1982 and in his day was the best left back in the world.

But I can't imagine myself ever quitting the Welsh squad because I was no longer first choice. I'll still be happy to be in the party when I'm thirty-three, even if it's just to help the younger lads come through, to play maybe half a game. Despite the bitter aftertaste of Prague, I still think there's no more exciting honour in soccer than playing for your country.

SUNDAY 6 DECEMBER

I've got my very own minder! Dennis Waterman, one of my favourite television actors, is sat with me in the bar at Gateshead Sports Centre where we've just finished taking part in a charity match. Now we're sipping a well-earned pint of lager each . . . or maybe it's the hair of the dog, because we had quite a few the night before.

With Juventus not having a game this weekend, I'd flown

back to England for thirty-six hours to take part in the game, which was organized by Steve Cram. Steve had jokingly asked Jim Pearson of Nike whether he could get me over. When Jim told me I jumped at the chance.

I've met Steve a couple of times, he's a smashing bloke with no airs or graces and he's a football fanatic, although he's had his problems supporting Sunderland! I was also delighted to get back, if only for a few hours, among people whom I could talk to.

Tracey came over with me, she spent the time visiting her parents while I went to the North East, one of my favourite football areas. The organisers had laid on a meal for the players the night before at the Tuxedo Princess, a floating nightclub moored on the River Tyne.

We had a lot of fun with people like Frank Bruno, Bobby Moore and Steve Coppell around. And there were a couple of lads from the Frankie Goes to Hollywood pop group there, who told me they'd agreed to play as soon as they knew I was coming because they were both ardent Liverpool supporters!

But Dennis Waterman was the star turn. I got on brilliantly with him, he was great fun and not a bit bigheaded or full of himself in any way. Mind, one of the lads knocked back so much drink he finished up asking the staff for the key to his cabin, thinking he was sleeping there!

I was really only there to kick off the game and take part in a penalty competition at half time. But once I got changed and out onto the pitch I couldn't resist staying on for twenty minutes.

Some of the show biz stars in our team actually asked me if I'd stay on awhile, just so they could talk about the time they played alongside Ian Rush. Dennis had insisted I play. 'You and me up front,' he said.

It's a strange thing, fame. I still find it difficult to come to terms with being a well-known figure, just because I happen to play football for a living. I look around me at people like Waterman, Bruno and Cram and think of them as being famous.

Yet they probably feel the same way as me, deep down most of the people who achieve some kind of fame through sport or show business are just ordinary folk at heart. Fame is something that's in the eye of the beholder. I've got a mum and dad, brothers and sisters back home who would soon shoot me down if I ever started getting any grand ideas!

Brendan Foster, who was refereeing the match, told me: 'You won't have to stay on long, I'll give your side a penalty and you can score with it, just to keep the crowd happy.' The penalty duly arrived and I missed it. I was clowning around, I toe-ended it . . . and it hit a post. I couldn't dare go off after that!

But I scored a goal a few minutes later, a nice low drive from the edge of the box. So I was happy to go off then, having shown the Geordies that I hadn't quite forgotten how to score.

The weekend without a serious game was a welcome break for me. To be perfectly honest, I hadn't been one hundred per cent fit all season. I'd had problems with my ankle for what seemed like an eternity. Most weeks I had barely been able to train. And before Juventus's games I would have a pain-killing injection, I was just struggling through game after game.

I knew it was wrong. I should have taken a good, long rest and allowed the injury to heal properly. But I was desperate to do well, to show all those people who were beginning to doubt that I was worth the money spent on me.

When I voiced my worries to Boniperti, he was equally keen on my continuing to play. We had a two-week break coming up at Christmas and that, he said, would really give me the chance to rest. So it was more injections when I arrived back in Turin, to prepare for the game I had looked forward to ever since the fixtures came out. Against Napoli and – Maradona.

SUNDAY 13 DECEMBER

The first thing you notice about Diego Maradona is how small he is. He looks no taller than my old pal Sammy Lee, who was just about the shortest player in the First Division during his days at Liverpool. But Maradona looks almost as wide as he is tall. The strength of those massive thighs shows he won't be easy to knock off the ball.

The real magic of the little man lies in his incredible ability to perform an art I've never seen on a football pitch before . . . to run without looking at the ball. You'll see what I mean if you study the video of that sensational goal he scored for Argentina against England in the World Cup.

The English defenders were blamed for not stopping him as he made that surging run into their penalty area. But the video shows he's not concentrating on the ball – he knows that is tied to his feet as if it was on a length of elastic. So he is able to watch for every lunging tackle, to ride them and be aware of the trail of defenders around him.

The coaching manuals could never teach any such skill . . . in fact it goes against everything you are ever taught. It's something that is nothing short of God-given. Indeed, it makes Maradona the greatest player in the world, greater even than Ruud Gullit, of whom I will talk later.

But for now my mind was on Maradona as 84,000 screaming supporters packing their stadium gave me a spine-chilling taste of football Neapolitan style. Mind, I'd already spent three days in our hotel on the outskirts of Naples finding out how fanatical those fans were.

Thousands of them had virtually laid siege to our hotel

from the moment we arrived. You couldn't walk near the door without a roar ringing out. If you attempted to sign a few autographs, you were mobbed. They were all friendly enough, in stark contrast to what I gather happened the previous season when hundreds drove their cars round the hotel all through the night, blaring their horns and making sure none of the Juventus players got any sleep!

This time they were good-natured, but you felt they wanted to be clinging onto you all the time. Our own Juventus fans are a passionate lot, but way down south it's something different again. Football, and in particular hero-worship of their stars, has been a way of life down there for as long as the game's been played. It will stay that way for the next one hundred years.

Those days before the game were depressing for me. I still couldn't shake off the feeling that some of our players were jealous of me, even envious of the attention the Naples fans were giving me. Maybe I'm a little bit sensitive, but I spent quite a lot of the time on my own.

However, it was no time for such sentiment once we walked out into that magnificent stadium. The huge crowd got behind their team from the kick-off, and Napoli, the reigning champions and already well on course to retain that title, hit us like bombs.

In the midst of it all, running the show, was Maradona. Normally a player who is prepared to run with the ball like he does will spend half his time in Italy on the ground and the other half on the treatment bench! But he's so good and so strong he can ride all the tackles that are lunging in at him right now.

He's all left foot, but those legs are so strong and powerful and he is brilliant at turning defenders inside out. He can go both ways with that left foot and there aren't too many players in the world who could do that. He's also crafty

enough to have learned the art of conning referees into award-
ing him a free kick even when he does lose the ball in a sliding
tackle.

A spectacular dive over that outstretched foot means you
normally win a free kick. I know ... I've won a few myself
that way in Italy! With all the pressure on us, we finally
concede a goal before the interval. But what a transformation
in the second half. With nothing to lose, we just went right
at them.

Suddenly it's Juventus who are looking the team at the top
of the table. We equalised and looked the team who were
going to win it. But then, with just a couple of minutes to
go, they won a penalty that was nothing short of diabolical
and that man Maradona calmly stepped up to ignore the
cauldron of noise and slot it home.

So we had been beaten, a defeat hard to swallow. But I'm
feeling reasonably encouraged as I sit down and reflect on
the game. Napoli are the best team in Italy right now and we
have shown we are as good as them. In fact, we've played
well against all the top teams. It's our results against the
lesser sides which have let us down.

WEDNESDAY 23 DECEMBER

Tracy and I have packed our bags – well, she has! We're
ready to drive to Turin airport, for a Christmas break at
home in Wales. Football closes down in Italy over the holiday
period and our next game is not until the new year.

We're both looking forward to being back with our families
and friends. It's been a wearying six months, getting used to
marriage and to the different customs, habits and lifestyle of
a foreign country. Laudrup told me it took him two years to
really begin to understand how to 'think' Italian, to understand the mentality as well as the language.

After six months, I've got mixed feelings. Our fans have been magnificent towards me and the man who owns Juventus, Gianni Agnelli, has been a great help. I've met him several times and every time we've spoken he's helped to build my confidence. When you're talking with him, it's hard to imagine that he is just about the most powerful man in all Italy.

He owns the Fiat company, whose annual turnover, so I'm told, exceeds £17 billion. He lives in a massive mansion near Villa Perosa, where we stay before our home games. We normally meet him in the grounds of his estate, where he has a friendly chat and words of advice and encouragement for all of us. Despite his fabulous wealth, he remains a football fan at heart and it shines through.

He is especially attentive towards me. He often has a ten-minute chat with the whole team and then ten minutes just talking to me. It's great to have him tell me how he still believes in me. Yet, ironically, I wonder if this is helping to cause a bit of resentment among some of the other players.

· SEVEN ·

Rude Awakening

MONDAY 28 DECEMBER

Christmas is over and the turkey's gone cold! I'm back in Turin and straight into a blazing row or as close as I can get to one, with our manager. Tracy and I had arrived back the previous night, having caught the seven o'clock plane from Heathrow – the only flight available that day.

I had even missed the christening of one of my nephews because I knew I had to be back for training today. Yet the newspapers are full of stories that I'm going to be fined five million lire (£2,500) because I'm late back. Marchesi was quoted as saying: 'I don't know where he is. He should be back here today (Sunday).'

I stormed into the ground, ignoring Marchesi at first and going straight to see the president, Boniperti. I'd learned by this time where the power really lay. If you had a grouse you went straight to the man at the top. I told him I was furious with the stories, that Marchesi had readily agreed to my coming back on the twenty-seventh and reporting for training the next day.

'That's all right,' said Boniperti, 'we won't be fining you.'

82

The same thing happened a few weeks earlier. One of the English papers had carried a story in which I was alleged to have threatened Juventus 'Drop me and I'll quit'. It was a load of rubbish, something I never said. But they'd threatened to fine me then, before I argued and won my case.

Now I don't want to sound like a moaner. If I've done something wrong, then I'll hold my hand up and take the punishment. But if I'm innocent, then I don't see why I should just sit back and take it. That's why I went in to see Marchesi from Boniperti's office, to get my feelings off my chest.

The guy's got problems. I am told by Italian journalists that managing an Italian football club must at times be an impossible mission. The demands for success every week appear to be enormous. Neither the manager nor the players can afford an 'off minute' never mind an 'off game'. I do not envy Marchesi his job at the moment.

As I've stated previously, Marchesi has been good to me in many ways, allowing me time off to visit my family. But we have never seen eye to eye on our ideas of the way football should be played. Maybe he was running scared, because he knew that another unsuccessful season would almost certainly mean the sack for him. But he was far too defensive-minded, he had the whole emphasis on defence even for home games.

But what used to make it even worse was that he would never take me to one side and tell me what he wanted. Instead I'd got used to reading in the newspapers such comments as: 'Rush must remember he's a defender when they have the ball, he must chase back'. Whenever I'd tackle him about it, he'd shrug his shoulders and deny ever making the statement! But it does cross my mind on occasion whether the Italian newspapers are wrong all the time.

Anyway, this particular day I'm ready for a real old barney.

But once again he shrugs those shoulders. 'You knew I wasn't due back for training until today so why have you blasted me all over the papers?' I asked. 'You know the papers ...' he answered. I believe he had said some strong words to them, to make it look in public as if he was taking a tough line with me.

I had already returned from the Christmas break determined to change my whole outlook on my job. I had reasoned that part of my problems so far was that I had not been forceful enough in my attitude. I'm still basically a shy person. Although by now my Italian is quite passable, I had still told people I couldn't speak the language, perhaps a bit nervous of making a fool of myself.

But over here everything's taken on face value. You ask an Italian if he can speak English and he'll answer 'Sure'. Then he'll proceed to spout the half dozen English words he actually knows! But he'll genuinely believe he's speaking perfect English. What's more, others will believe him, too.

It seeems to me, Italian players are also a far more self-centred breed than those I'd grown up with at Liverpool. Football is supposed to be a team game, but we had players more interested in themselves. That applies both on and off the pitch. If you act like a star you'll be treated like one.

At Liverpool, the lads would have you up against a brick wall for strutting about the way some of our players did. But if you can't beat the system, you've got to join it and I'm grimly determined to look after myself more from now on. I can't ever imagine me acting flash, but I'm going to show that I'm not going to be shoved around any more.

My argument against Marchesi, that spending my time charging back to help our defence would not help me or the team, is not based on selfishness, anyway. If I'm forced to go looking for the ball, it means that others in the team are not doing their job, supplying the openings they're supposed to create for their strikers.

I guess I've got what's called a goal scorer's mentality. I'm blinkered in some ways, scoring goals is *the* all-important facet of my game. I've never been the world's best in the air, for instance, and going back to mark their centre half at corners would probably land me and my team in more trouble than it's worth.

Yet if there's a chance of a goal, something gets inside me and gets me that precious few extra inches off the ground. Don't ask me what, it's just pure instinct. I remember one of my better headed goals for Liverpool against Leicester a year or two back. Although their centre half was a good few inches taller than me I got up higher and it needed only a touch to go in.

Gary Gillespie said to me later: 'If that had been on the halfway line, you'd never have won the ball. You only won it because you could smell a goal.' He was dead right. Some people might criticize me for it, but then they used to hand the same flak out to Jimmy Greaves for doing next to nothing until the ball was in the penalty area. He wasn't half bad then, though!

SUNDAY 3 JANUARY 1988

And a welcome start to the new year. We've gained a good 2–2 draw against our bitter local rivals Torino in their 'home' match, even though both fixtures are played in the same stadium.

I've scored our second equalizer, six or seven minutes from time, to send our half of the huge crowd home happy. It came when Laudrup went down the wing, cut the ball back and I got there a fraction before a defender to touch it in. So I'm well pleased ... even if some of the reporters are putting it down as an own goal.

SUNDAY 10 JANUARY

Last week I was a hero, this time I'm slaughtered by the press. I missed a couple of chances I would normally expect to tuck away and we've been beaten 1–0 at home by A C Milan. 'No good, the Worst Player!' was one headline the following day. But what's far worse is that I feel hostility in our own dressing room.

Nothing was actually said to my face, I'd have much preferred it if it was. I don't mind a stand-up row. But I can just feel that some of my colleagues were blaming me. You could cut the atmosphere in our dressing room with a knife. I felt I hadn't played badly, I was in the right position for the chances and both were saved well by their goalkeeper.

Milan at this stage of the season were beginning to mount a championship surge. Ruud Gullit, who had already established a massive reputation since his move from Holland, scored the only goal, a dynamic header in the second half.

It was my first view of Gullit and he's so big, so muscular and so powerful he's almost like a monster in football boots! But he's blessed with tremendous skill and balance for such a big man. Imagine one of those great big British centre halves with the touch of Glenn Hoddle and you'll get an impression of the man.

With his pace as well, he's just about unstoppable when he embarks on those surging runs into the opposition penalty area. Certainly today we had nobody to hold him. Brio is our toughest and strongest defender but he was out injured. So poor Bruno had the job of marking Gullit. Brave and determined as he was – and he handled the Dutchman pretty well on the ground – he just had no chance of stopping him in the air.

Impressed as I was by Gullit, I don't think he's quite in the Maradona class. The little Argentinian is out on his own as the number one player in the world. He is a man who can win a game with one flashing stroke of brilliance. Yet Gullit is probably the better team player.

He would blend into any team, anywhere in the world. And you could play him in just about any position. I must say I'd love the chance of lining up alongside him one day. His willingness to work, as well as add the class touches to Milan has made them, to my mind, the best team in Italy right now. I stress the word *team*.

To me, they were the only side we had faced who seemed to have built up that all-important team spirit and ability to knit together as a single unit. Every team in our league has its stars, there are dozens of great individual players. But Milan had stars who were prepared to put their talents towards the good of the whole team. That's why I fancy them strongly to climb past Napoli and win the League.

WEDNESDAY 20 JANUARY

When a striker really clicks, he's living in dreamland, in a wonderful world where he knows he's likely to score with every touch. I've just had one of those thrilling experiences. Yet I'm sat in the dressing room at Pescara still feeling angry and sore. For I've just scored four goals – and then been substituted!

'You have scored too many goals already tonight. You need to save some for Como on Sunday,' Marchesi told me when he pulled me off twenty-five minutes from the end. I was going crazy. 'You can't go trying to spread a player's goals round. They come when they come,' I protested.

But it was to no avail. Buzo, our teenage reserve striker, came on for me and promptly missed a couple of sitters. I was reckoning on finishing the game with half a dozen, so confident was I feeling. In the end I walked disconsolately into our dressing room and missed the last few minutes of the game.

Laudrup scored the two other goals in our 6–2 win, which took us to the quarter finals of the Italian Cup. We had struggled to beat Pescara in the home leg of the tie 1–0 and I got the goal. But this night we really did show the country that Juventus, for all their inconsistencies in the League, were far from a spent force.

I went right through the repertoire with my goals. The first was a header, the second a right-footer from the edge of the box, the third a long-range effort with my left foot and the fourth a simple tap-in. The players all congratulated me when they joined me in the dressing room. Some, like Brio and Tacconi, really made me feel like a hero. But one or two of the others weren't quite so forthcoming. Nothing you could put your finger on, but just that feeling that things weren't quite right.

The next day the newspapers, who have been giving me some unmerciful hammer, are singing my praises again and Marchesi is taking some stick for pulling me off. His actions still didn't make any sense to me. If he'd told me he just wanted to save me from getting injured I could have at least accepted it.

But goals are the lifeblood of a centre forward and I certainly needed all I could get. The more you score the more you build up your confidence. When you're scoring regularly you reach a stage where you actually expect to score in every game. I've had that feeling in my days at Liverpool and it does breed success.

Mind, I'm probably public enemy number one as far as

Pescara are concerned. In three league and cup games against them I've banged in seven goals. They're talking of bringing in a monk before we play them in the league again next month – to pray for their deliverance! Even Maradona would struggle against that kind of opposition. . . .

SUNDAY 31 JANUARY

Another 'first' for me, as I score from the penalty spot in our 4–0 win over Empoli. We were a couple of goals up when we were awarded the penalty and a few of the players urged me to take it. Mauro, our little right winger, was one of them. And I'm not sure how pleased he really was when I scored. He was one of the players who I could never work out.

Maybe he felt he was the man to take over the mantle of superstar after Michel Platini left them at the end of last season. He's not a bad player, a good, tricky runner, but he's inclined to be selfish. Surely anyone with vision would be delighted to play to my strengths rather than deny me the ball all the time.

Still, I'm feeling quite good in myself by this stage of the season. The injuries which plagued my time up to Christmas have thankfully cleared up and I believe I'm playing pretty well. But it's still hard to come to terms with the Italian temperament and mentality. When I score a goal, the first thing I want to do is to shake the hand of the man who made it for me.

But the others are only concerned in putting on a one-man show for the supporters. Maybe coming from a perfect team like Liverpool, where everybody played as a team-player, has spoiled me. At Anfield, players praised you for every good pass. Here it counts for nothing. You can't help wondering at times: Why bother to be unselfish? Nobody seems to appreciate it.

· EIGHT ·

Saints and Sinners

WEDNESDAY 3 FEBRUARY

The news I'd feared from back home for the past couple of months finally broke today. Mike England has been sacked as manager of Wales. I can't help feeling that it was, partly at least, my fault. If I hadn't missed three chances against Czechoslovakia in Prague back last year, we would have qualified for the European Championship finals and he would have been a hero.

Now he's out. I telephoned him at his home to tell him how sorry I was. To my mind it is a terrible decision by the FA of Wales. Before Mike took over in 1980, Wales were a third-rate footballing nation. Now he had turned them into a team to be feared, one which could hold its own against the very best.

Mike had a great talent for spotting young players and giving them their chance. He had me in his squad when I was only eighteen and hadn't played a single first-team game for Liverpool. He's told me since that many of the committee members were against my call-up because I was so young and inexperienced. But he always believed in his young players.

The senior players in the Welsh squad had actually threatened to go on strike if Mike was sacked. That was in the heat of the moment after our disappointment in Prague. And by now we had realized that taking that kind of action would only bring further harm to our national team. But the affair still left a bitter taste in my mouth.

It seems to me that the one thing Mike never had was that precious little bit of luck at the right time. I only hope that will change for the new manager. I reckon that, with my twenty-seventh birthday coming up in October, I've only got one chance left of playing in the World Cup finals. That's the dream of every footballer – but time is running out for me.

As for the FA of Wales, they were to make fools out of themselves in the following couple of weeks, with a different manager seemingly being drummed out every day – all turning them down. Brian Clough, Terry Venables, Bob Paisley. . . they were all asked and said no.

Mind you Cloughie would have been an intriguing choice. Everyone has very definite views about him – they either love him or hate him. I think I would have enjoyed the experience of playing for Wales under him, for a few days at a time. But for the week-in week-out grind, I think I'd prefer the low-key Liverpool way.

Whether he really wanted to take the job is something only he knows, despite the frequent claims that he was interested. Deep down, I think the job he's really yearned for is England manager. I'm sure he'd do a great job for them too. But with his personality he's never going to get the chance. He's always ready to spell out the truth and damn the consequences. That's not the way the FA likes to see things done.

By now, I'm speaking Italian with much more confidence,

even using the lingo to answer questions from the local pressmen. It also means, of course, that I can understand the language that bit better and some of the things that are in the papers horrify me.

Unnamed team-mates were being quoted having a real go at me, complaining that I wasn't trying on the field, that I was a loner and a misery off it. When I angrily questioned them the reporters who wrote the stories refused to tell me who had given them the quotes. In the dressing room players would just shrug their shoulders and say they knew nothing.

As is often the way in such matters, there is no one that I know of who I can really accuse of speaking out of turn, however, I feel uncomfortable not because of anything the player's say to me to take offence at but just because I feel a bit of an atmosphere. Some days it would be fine, with everybody eager to say hello. Then the very next day, they'd totally ignore me.

Maybe some of it's down to me for not trying to dominate the dressing room. In Italy, when you're built up as a superstar, you have to play like one and act like one. I'm just a normal guy, I can't go around telling the world how good I am. But I suspect that is what they really want me to do.

The newspapers wanted another Platini, who had become a celebrity both on and off the field before leaving Juventus last season. In the end, he won the people of Turin over. Yet even he had a rough ride when he first moved there. Italy had just won the World Cup and six of the Juventus side were in that team.

They apparently resented the introduction of the Frenchman into a side which had also just won the Italian Championship – he was frozen out for months. In fact there is a story that he may have been involved in a scuffle with a team-mate in the dressing room. At least nobody's tried to pick a stand-up fight with me yet. But in a way I'd prefer that.

Anything's better than the mental torment I am going through.

Mind, the newspapers back home in England were doing their fair share towards dragging me down. One story which particularly incensed me was written by Trevor Francis, telling me to stop moaning and enjoy all the money I was making. Who on earth is he to start shouting his mouth off? As far as I can recall he spent more of his time in Italy injured than he ever did playing.

I'll bet that by the end of my first season I'll have probably played as many games as he did in all his time in Italy. He never played for one of the high-profile, high-pressure clubs either. Sampdoria are a good side nowadays, but they weren't when he was there. He never had to live in the kind of goldfish bowl I'm having to.

Francis doesn't even need the money to write rubbish like this. I just can't understand him. Even Paul Rideout, whose experience of Italy was limited to the Second Division, had a go. It's a pity some folk don't concern themselves more with their own lives.

Jimmy Greaves had also been saying on television that I should cut my losses and get back home as quickly as I could. Now, while I disagree, I can at least accept Jimmy's words as being well-meaning. After all, he suffered a pretty torrid time himself in Italy, he went through real trauma and he was handing out advice through genuine feeling.

SUNDAY 28 FEBRUARY: ROME

No, I haven't been to visit Pope John-Paul, which must remain an ambition as yet unfulfilled. But I've enjoyed the next best thing, in the form of two English priests from the Vatican who have come to visit me in our hotel. They're both big football supporters, so they came to ask for a couple of tickets for our match against Roma. That's one request I daren't refuse!

We sat for quite a while drinking coffee and talking. They gave me a fascinating insight into the way the Vatican is run. They even have priests' soccer teams there. These two play in a combined United Kingdom team against priests from other countries and right old kicking matches they are too, so they tell me!

I'll bet there's a long queue to the confessional box after the games! But, as a Catholic, I'm intrigued to hear about it all, to see the human side of a place as grand as the Vatican.

Mind, I knew already that the Pope was an ardent football supporter. Somewhere in his private residence there's an autographed picture of me! It all came about last year when Sister Winefride, a nun who had taught at my old school St Richard Gwyn in Flint, visited Lourdes and chatted to a priest from the Vatican who was on a pilgrimage.

Somehow the topic got around to football and when she mentioned she was from the same town as myself the priest asked her if she could arrange for me to send a picture to the Pope. I could hardly believe it when she came back and told me. I had to go round to my local church to ask Canon Andrews how I should sign it. I could hardly write 'Yours in Sport' or 'Good luck. . . .'

He told me that 'Your Eminence' was the right way to address the Pope. So that's what I signed in the end. I also had to send one off to one of the Archbishops in Italy, I think it was Milan. That had to be signed 'Your Grace'. Well, when you're giving your autograph to such illustrious people, you have to be a stickler for accuracy!

It's strange and mind-boggling really how people who are so much more eminent and more important than you can still value a thing like an autograph. There is no doubt in my mind about the 'Greatest' supporter I've ever had and I use that word to describe her rather than me.

It was Sister Benigne, a wonderful lady from Liverpool who had become a nun in Lourdes many years ago. Yet she remained an ardent Liverpool supporter. When a man I knew from Flint went over to Lourdes to do some decorating, he found cuttings of me on her apartment walls.

He told her he knew me, and she asked him if I could send an autographed picture for her. We wrote back and fore to each other regularly after that before sadly she died last year. I have my own picture of her, signed 'To my wonder footballer'. It brings a lump to my throat every time I see it.

Incidentally, all this support didn't help my cause much against Roma. We lost 2–0! But Rome is still a wonderful city and you never know who you're likely to bump into there. Singer Joe Cocker was staying in our hotel, so I had a few drinks with him after the game. He's a big soccer fan, too, and he can talk about the game in fluent English!

· NINE ·

Familiar Feelings

WEDNESDAY 23 MARCH: SWANSEA

I'm back in Wales, to play against Yugoslavia in a friendly international, our first since that sad exit from the European Championships. There's a sparse crowd at the Vetch Field to see us lose 2–1, after going ahead through Dean Saunders early on.

After all their futile efforts to land a big-name new manager, the FA of Wales still haven't come up with anybody, so David Williams, a coach at Norwich, is in temporary charge. To be honest, we didn't play well – the hangover from Prague was still with us.

But it's interesting being back in Britain to see all the newspapers speculating about whether I'll be coming back for good in a few months time. As usual, the reporters seem to know far more about what's going on than the player! As far as I'm concerned, I'm perfectly prepared to see out my three year contract at Juventus.

I'd be lying if I said I was completely happy. Just a couple of days with the Welsh squad, all the fun, the chat and the mickey-taking, makes me realize how much I'm missing back in Turin. But I didn't expect life to be a bed of roses when I signed that contract. It will make me a wealthy man and I've got to give them something back for that. And there is at least one man I want to succeed for. Mr Agnelli, the man who owns half of Italy or so it seems, has steadfastly kept faith with me.

He continues to build up my confidence whenever we meet and that's quite often. There's even talk of another British player being brought in to play alongside me next season or maybe a couple, if the Italian FA agree to raise the number of foreign players per team from two to three.

Since the new year, I've been reasonably satisfied with my own form, although the team have fallen away a little bit and are struggling to stay in touch with the top half dozen sides in the league. As far as the language is concerned, I'm confident and fluent enough by now to actually take part in television interviews in Italian. So that's a big breakthrough.

We had also scrambled through to the semi-finals of the Italian Cup, drawing 1–1 away to Avelino and scraping a 1–0 win in the home leg. So that had given us the chance of a different route back to Europe next season.

Yet goals continue to be everything to the press and because I'm not scoring as regularly as I'd have liked, I'm getting murdered. If I'm seen out at night having a meal with Tracy, then I'm reported as being drunk. If I stay at home, then I'm a misery who shuns everybody and lives on baked beans! You just can't win against this lot.

Luckily Tracy is sensible enough to ignore all the nonsense and she's been a tremendous help to me. I know I make life difficult for her at times. Some days I'd come home from the ground really pleased and happy, because it seemed I'd finally began to be accepted by the other players.

Then the very next day things would all turn sour again. I'd be home with a black mood and she would have to suffer for it. Yet she was probably going through a more traumatic time than me. At least I had my football to fall back on.

Our personal lives were not helped when things started appearing in the newspapers, supposedly about our private life. Mr Lucca, our landlord, was also getting on my nerves more and more. Because I wouldn't allow him to run my life, to tell me where to eat, who to go with, where to be seen, the atmosphere between us was not very good.

There were crazy stories about Tracy and myself having screaming matches, of me even hitting her. It was all total nonsense. Sure, we've had our rows like any other married couple. But nothing remotely resembling the pitched battles the papers claimed. Who was feeding them all this rubbish I'll never know for sure.

It might sound as though I'm becoming almost paranoid, but I'm even believing that the telephone in my apartment is bugged. Just about everyone who calls tells me there's a strange buzz at my end of the line. Even when I make local calls, the line is very faint and blurred.

I would put nothing past some of the people I have come across in my time in Italy. We've made some real, true friends, but I'm sick and tired of the hangers-on, who promise you everything and deliver nothing. If you score a goal you're a hero and they want to latch onto you. If you go a couple of weeks without a goal, you don't even see them.

The future of our manager is looking in more doubt with every passing week as our form continues to be erratic. The papers are already beginning their guessing game of who the new manager will be next season. Marchesi seems to be almost resigned to his fate. He's a nice bloke, and I can't help feeling sorry for him. Yet there is a growing lack of respect for him within the dressing room.

It's becoming increasingly obvious that something will have to be done. If only he'd change his ways, and make us more positive on the field. But I'm not sure whether we'd have the players to transform our style or whether some of the players even care. For some of them know that they'll be on their bikes come the end of the season.

I continue to get regular telephone calls from Kenny Dalglish and Graeme Souness, which are a great help to me. If I score a goal, Kenny will be on the phone the next day to say well done and to keep offering me encouragement.

Graeme is the same. He's played in Italy, so he knows all the problems and his advice is tremendously useful. I know that the cynics may believe that both were acting after their own interests – Rangers have already been linked with me, as well as Liverpool, Everton and Manchester United.

But I can say with all honesty that neither of them ever mentioned the possibility of my joining their clubs. It was all down to friendship. After all, I'd played alongside the two of them and they were only too pleased to pass on to me the benefit of their greater experience.

Those calls have helped me get through many a long winter's night. In particular, a video Kenny sent over kept me warm. It was a compilation of Liverpool's greatest moments, including all the trophies they'd collected while I was there. Watching film clips of some of the goals I scored made me realize I wasn't such a bad player after all and made me determined that I could do it again.

SUNDAY 10 APRIL: ASCOLI

Today is a perfect example of what I mean about goals being all-important in Italy. I've just put on probably my worst performance since I joined Juventus – could hardly do a thing right. Yet I somehow poked in the equalizer to give us a 1–1 draw.

Now the reporters are telling me what a great game I had!

It will be all over the newspapers in the morning, too. I just give them a wry smile when they crowd round me. I just wonder what they would have been saying and reporting if I hadn't been in the right spot to grab that goal. . . .

TUESDAY 12 APRIL: LEEDS

I really feel I'm back in the old routine – I've just scored a hat trick against Everton! Not for Liverpool this time, but for Leeds United, in a Testimonial Match for John Charles and Bobby Collins. Boniperti, a longtime friend of Big John, had asked me if I would play and I was only too delighted to say yes.

Charles is certainly the greatest Welsh footballer of all time and maybe the best of any nationality. He was also, of course, a living legend as far as Juventus were concerned, having blazed the trail from Britain and Italy more than thirty years ago and then smashed the club's goalscoring records. I'd also met him a few times and found him to be a really genuine, unspoilt man, which made me want to help him all the more.

I flew over to Manchester Airport the day before because I wanted to get my hair cut while I was in England and my local hairdresser in Liverpool remains the best I've ever known! I stayed at an hotel on the outskirts of Leeds on the night before the match. The first person I met the following morning was Geoff Boycott.

He was attending some function there, but he came over and introduced himself. He then introduced me to a friend with him, declaring: 'This is Ian Rush, he used to score goals!' He then gave me a fair old bit of flak and some constructive advice on my problems.

I didn't mind what he said at all. Boycott is perhaps one of the most controversial men in all sport, certainly cricket, but nine times out of ten what he says is right. He might have been called dead selfish as a batsman, but for all that he was one of the best ever. Every team in the world would have wanted him at his peak, simply because he was the best.

If they ever played cricket in Italy, he would have been an absolute god over there. He knows how to look after himself, how to organize his life and how to get the supporters rooting for him. Maybe he would have had the establishment tearing their hair, but the man in the street, the ordinary fan, would have loved him.

John Charles came in soon afterwards and he had a chat with me as well. He appreciated that in his days at Juventus, when he scored more than one hundred goals in five seasons, they were a great team. But even he had his problems off the field, with people wanting to run his life for him. He just told me to keep battling away, to keep my head up, and the goals would come.

We were off to a testimonial lunch before the game, where I planned to spend an hour at most and then slip out quietly and get back to the hotel for an afternoon's rest. Some hope! In the end I was there until well after half past four, waiting for Platini – one of the other guest players in Leeds' team – to make his appearance.

He didn't show up at all at the lunch, sending a message that his plane – and I mean *his*, it's his personal jet – had been late arriving and he had headed straight to the hotel for a rest. By this time Bernard Manning, the guest speaker, had been on his feet for some two hours. He told me earlier he was only going to crack a few jokes for twenty minutes!

He showed what a true professional he is. I know that a lot of people don't appreciate his acid humour and sure, he can be a bit vindictive. But he takes the mickey out of himself more than out of anyone else. He didn't mind a few cracks made by others at his expense either. He might dish out the vitriol – but he can take it as well.

By the time I got back to the hotel, I only had time for a quick bath before coming downstairs to meet my dad, who had come across from Flint with a few of his pals to see the game. I had a cup of tea with them, then it was off to Elland Road to meet up with Platini, Scirea (one of my current team-mates at Juventus), and Kenny Dalglish, who were all guesting for Leeds with me.

I'd met Platini before, because he had been to Juventus a few times to train with us. He kept himself to himself in the dressing room. But what really cheered me was the sight of Kenny changing alongside me. It really was just like the old days. We had a chat, but he mentioned nothing about the game.

I could tell by his mood, though, how seriously he was taking it all. A testimonial or a cup final, he'd be the same before any game. There were more than 15,000 people who had paid to watch and they deserved to be rewarded by seeing players taking the game seriously. That was his philosophy.

Everton had their strongest available team out, so they were taking it seriously. And they showed that by their tackling in the first few minutes. It was as fierce as in any League game. I found myself drifting back in the early stages, just like I had become used to doing at Juventus. But Dalglish quickly ordered me back up front.

I didn't need any second request to get back to my old role. And it didn't take long for me to appreciate even more the value of having Kenny alongside me. I had the ball just outside the Everton penalty area and I was going to try a hopeful long shot when I heard that familiar Scottish brogue: 'One-two'.

All I heard was the call. I didn't even look up to see him. I didn't have to. It was just like the old days. I just shoved the ball in the direction of the voice and hurtled forward. The ball was suddenly back at my feet – and Everton's defence was torn apart. All I had to do was run on and then slot it past Neville Southall.

How many times over the years have I scored that kind of goal, from that kind of pass, from the same man? I wouldn't even care to guess. In fact, Kenny must have been instrumental in a pretty large percentage of all the goals I ever scored for Liverpool. Now we're back together and it's like we've never been apart.

The amazing thing about it is that we've never once, in all those years, actually discussed tactics with each other. People think we spent hours together practising our moves, planning our strategy. Yet I don't think we ever gave it so much as a thought. Some might call it a kind of mental telepathy, but all that talk's way above my head. As far as I'm concerned we're both instinctive footballers and we have always thought on that same wavelength.

If my first goal followed a touch of vintage Dalglish, it was Platini who took over the show from that stage. He made my second goal with one of the greatest passes I've ever received – a chip with backspin that left the Everton defenders stranded and virtually stopped invitingly in my path.

Poor Southall was left totally exposed again. I couldn't resist selling him an outrageous dummy by pretending to shoot. As he dived headlong I just lifted the ball over him and to the gaping goal behind him. All goalkeepers hate being made to look a bit of a mug and Neville is such a dedicated, single-minded pro he's affected worse than anyone.

I knew he was wild with me. He was even angrier when I completed my hat trick early in the second half, again from a pass by Platini. The little Frenchman was playing superbly. In fact, I reckon he's still good enough to be playing at top level. I'd have dearly loved to have had someone with his passing ability playing with me at Juventus.

Not that I blame him for retiring at the end of last season. He's got a top television job in France, plenty of money. Apparently he was given plenty of stick by the Italian press last year, even though it was not his fault that the club struggled. He was making the passes but there was nobody to get on the end of them.

Poor Southall – who I happen to believe is the best goal-keeper in the world – had seen enough of me. He made a great save from me, pushing the ball behind for a corner. As I came into his area he looked up and said: 'Why don't you ... off back to Italy!' I just burst out laughing. Well, we are mates in the Welsh team. I *think* he was joking. . . .

It's back to Italy the next morning. But in style this time, in Platini's jet. The game had been shown live on Italian television, so I knew my goals would have caused a stir. I'd been going through a lean spell with Juventus, so I was delighted that the supporters had been shown that, given the right service, I can still score goals.

· TEN ·

On the Spot

Our biggest League game of the season has just ended in triumph. We've hammered Napoli 3–1 and sent our packed crowd home delirious with our best performance of the whole year. I scored our second goal – a near-post left footer from Di Agostini's low cross. The only sour spot came when we scored our third goal, from a penalty.

As I walked back to the centre circle, I was staggered to see our Captain Cabrini trudging disconsolately from the field. He had already been booked earlier and now he had been sent off. We discovered later it was for arguing with the referee. I've never heard in my life before of a player being dismissed as his side scored.

Well as we played, the game confirmed my feelings that Napoli were not the best side in Italy any more. This defeat, in fact, marked the start of their slide down the table and allowed Milan – and Ruud Gullit – to overhaul them. Maradona had a quiet game, doing next to nothing apart from making their goal near the end. Yet still the papers were to praise him the next day. 'Without Maradona defeat would have been even more overwhelming,' said one. As I've stated before, when you're the king in this country you never lose your crown!

Even in the glow of such a victory, there is no kind of celebration after the game. The players just get changed and disappear their various ways, as usual. There is no players' lounge like all the major English clubs have.

I'm going out for a drink and a meal with Bruno later. But I still feel a little empty as I dress and head off to meet Tracy. I love football, but I love the fun and the friendships off the field too. They just don't exist here, apart from a precious few people. Bruno and Brio are both great guys, Tacconi is still a bubbling inspiration. But I can barely remember any of the others doing as much as asking me out for dinner.

WEDNESDAY 20 APRIL

We're out of the Italian Cup and almost certainly out of Europe next season. For a club like Juventus such a prospect is unthinkable. It's twenty-five years since they last failed to qualify for at least one of the European competitions. So the mood in our dressing room is one of abject despair.

We've actually beaten Torino 2–1 on the night, but have lost the semi-final to our bitter rivals on a 3–2 aggregate as they'd beaten us 2–0 in the first leg. What makes it all the more sickening is that we could so easily have romped through to the final. We murdered them and could have scored a bagful. But I hit the woodwork, as did a couple of other efforts from our side.

We are languishing in seventh spot in the League, which means we've got to improve if we are to win a UEFA Cup spot. Our only real hope is that Sampdoria go on to beat Torino in the Cup Final and we can sneak past our local rivals in the table. But they're a couple of points ahead of us with precious few games left to play. It's going to be tough.

WEDNESDAY 27 APRIL: STOCKHOLM

Another disaster for Wales, as we crash 4–1 to a powerful Swedish team already being hailed as the rising new stars of Europe. It's the first game in charge for Terry Yorath – an appointment I welcomed because I'd been in the squad with him during his playing days and knew what a devoted and proud Welshman he was.

But it's an unhappy first game for Yorath. He tried to introduce some new tactics, playing Mark Hughes, Dean Saunders and myself up front, leaving our midfield under-manned. He also told our defenders to hold their positions and the result was that the Swedes were allowed to run straight through us.

At least this was only a friendly, so defeat wasn't the end of the world. We had a long chat about the way we played after the game and Terry was big enough to accept that his tactics were wrong. Everybody learns by mistakes and the best place to put new ideas into practice, to experiment, is away from the pressures of the World Cup or the European Championships.

SUNDAY 1 MAY

What a topsy-turvy season this is proving to be. We've just beaten our old enemies Torino 2–1 in our last but one home game of the season. Suddenly the door to Europe is wide open again. It takes us level on points with them, with just two more games to go. It looks as if whichever side finishes ahead will clinch that last UEFA Cup spot.

To make it even better, I scored the winner just a couple

of minutes from the end, taking a pass with my back to goal, dummying to go one way and then turning the other to hit it with my left foot, a dozen yards out. It was a sweet moment. Yet I seem to have the knack of managing something special in derby games. I always seemed to do extra well whenever Liverpool played Everton.

Thousands of our fans were still waiting outside the ground as I left and they tried to carry me out in triumph! I'd got used to our passionate supporters by now. I really loved them and played for them. I could even talk to them in their own language, which they loved.

Because I didn't make a big fuss about it in our dressing room, though, I'm sure that most of my team-mates were unaware that I could now more than hold my own in conversation in their language. If I'd been like this from the day I arrived, maybe things might have been so much different.

Perhaps the biggest mistake Juventus made was not bringing in an interpretor for me. I'm sure that would have helped me become conversant in Italian so much more quickly. They expected Laudrup to act as my unofficial translator. He didn't do a great deal. But I can understand his point of view. He had his own life to live, his own problems to sort out. He wasn't having a very happy season and had enough on his plate looking after himself. Having been there longer than me, he knew only too well that if you don't act for yourself nobody will.

SUNDAY 15 MAY

How to make a disaster out of success – I reckon Juventus could outdo any team in the fiasco stakes. Our last League game of the season has been a real letdown, we've lost 2–1 at home to Fiorentina. It's galling to find out afterwards that only a draw would have been enough to virtually guarantee ourselves a place in Europe.

Now, with Torino also losing, we've finished in level sixth spot in the table, behind champions AC Milan, Napoli, Sampdoria, Roma and Inter Milan. So we have to pray that our rivals lose the Italian Cup final. That looks a fair bet as they're down 2–0 already to Sampdoria after the first leg. If they don't pull back the deficit, it means that we'll have to face them for an incredible fifth time in a season with the winners earning the final European qualifying position.

MONDAY 16 MAY

No time to mope over our Euro-worries because I'm on the early morning plane back to England and then on the shuttle north to take part in a testimonial match for my old Liverpool mate Alan Hansen. It will feel strange pulling on a Liverpool shirt again for the first time in a year.

The opposition isn't bad, though. It's the England squad who are using the game as an important warm-up in their preparations for the forthcoming European Championship finals in West Germany. I'm looking forward to seeing a lot of real old friends, but I don't know what the mood of the players will be.

They've just been beaten in the FA Cup Final by Wimbledon which stopped them winning the League and Cup double. Having watched the final on television back in Italy, I know they won't be happy with the way they played. It was nowhere near their best. Poor John Aldridge will still be haunted by that penalty miss. I feel for him more than anyone.

I'd been invited to take part in the game the week before. Hansen discovered I was coming over to play in a testimonial game for Frank Stapleton on the Tuesday so he telephoned and asked if I could stop off at Anfield en route. I was only too pleased to agree. But first he had to get permission off Dalglish. Kenny had warned that no outsiders could play, he wanted the game taken seriously. But he made an exception for me.

There were thousands of supporters milling around when I arrived at the ground. It was heartwarming to hear them chant my name. It was good to see the Liverpool lads again, although they were still a little depressed about the Cup Final. But it was when I walked onto the pitch that it really hit me that I was back 'home' again.

The 31,552 supporters packed into the ground gave me a fantastic welcome. It brought a lump to my throat as they chanted 'Rushie is back!' and 'Do you want to come back home?' They even had some advice for Dalglish: 'Kenny, Kenny, bring him back'.

I was on the bench to start the game, as Kenny played the eleven who had been in the Cup Final – the right thing to do in the circumstances. I came on after half an hour for Peter Beardsley . . . and spent the next fifteen minutes embarrassing myself!

I didn't bother to warm up before I came on. So I could barely stand up, never mind hold the ball. The game was going on around me at what seemed breakneck speed and I just couldn't keep up with it at all. I felt such a mug, especially after all that build-up from the fans.

But by the second half I was warmed up. Dalglish came on alongside me, to really lift the whole team. We were losing 1–0 at half-time, but then Kenny took over. He sent me surging through after two pin point passes and I scored both times – at the Kop End, too. The fans went wild and I savoured every moment, having the crowd virtually breathing down your neck.

At the Juventus stadium the supporters are some twenty

yards further back and the volume of noise just doesn't hit you the same way. I believe that players respond to the crowd. The more noise, the more atmosphere, the better you play.

We won the game 3–2, which gave me a lot of satisfaction. But my real feelings as I walked off the pitch were for those fantastic supporters. There had been a lot of talk about me coming back home, with half a dozen British clubs linked with me.

Even before the match, hordes of fans were imploring me not to join Everton, one of the interested clubs. I knew by the end of the game that if I was to come back it would have to be to Liverpool. They'd never have forgiven me for moving to another club back over here, and I doubt if I could have lived with myself either.

I wasn't quite so sure a couple of hours later, however, when I finished up with pie in my face at Hansen's Testimonial Dinner! I guess I had it coming, mind. At my leaving party a year before I'd squashed a pie in the face of Kenny Dalglish's wife Marina. I knew she was thirsting for revenge.

She'd already got her own back before my last game in England for Liverpool, at Chelsea. She managed to get hold of my suitcase while we were training, taken my tie, emptied two pounds of sugar into the case and, put itching powder all over my best shirt.

I was on the Saint and Greavsie show, live on television, that lunchtime. I had to borrow a tie and my shirt was making me itch like mad all the way to the studio. Ian St John and Jimmy Greaves must have thought I was lousy!

At least I managed to stop myself from scratching during the interview. But I knew then that you're asking for trouble if you cross Marina Dalglish! Now I was still wary, still waiting for more revenge from her.

But I let my guard slip for just a few seconds as we sat at

the table. That was enough ... suddenly all I could see is this big, creamy pie heading for me. It was too late to duck. Just about everybody in the room had been waiting for the moment, so an almighty cheer went up. Welcome back to Liverpool, Ian!

I scored again the next day in Dublin, where I had a good, long chat with Paul Gascoigne, the fast emerging star from Newcastle. A smashing, lively lad he is too, no edge at all, just one of the boys. He likes his pint or two as well. He sounds just right for Liverpool!

Best news of the week, though, came from Italy. Torino had lost in the Cup Final, despite taking the second leg of the tie into extra time. So it meant a death or glory finale against them next week.

For the winners there was sixth spot in the table and a place in the UEFA Cup. For the losers ... only ignominy. For a club as big and as powerful as Juventus, a club who regarded a place in Europe almost as their divine right, defeat would be nothing short of humiliation. We just couldn't lose this one – we dare not.

MONDAY 23 MAY

Play-off day at last, after what seems an eternity of waiting. The newspapers have built up the game into something approaching a world war, but the match itself is a real battle of attrition. There was so much tension – and perhaps a lot of tiredness as well after a long season – that neither side came remotely close to scoring, even after extra time.

So it's a penalty shoot-out. And I'm named fifth taker in our team, the spot most people reckon is the ultimate test of nerves. I do have the comfort of knowing that Juventus had never lost a game in which I'd scored – I'd carried on that long record I had at Liverpool.

Nevertheless, it's nerve-jangling watching the others take their penalties. We missed one early on, but Torino then missed with their third and fourth kicks. So I stepped up knowing that if I scored they couldn't catch us and the proud twenty-five year run in Europe would be maintained.

Strangely, all the nerves left me as I stepped forward. It was comforting to know that even if I missed they still had to score to stay alive. I struck my shot right-footed to the left side of the goal as I looked at it. The goalkeeper dived the right way, but the shot glanced off the inside of the post and into the net.

Just a couple of inches wider and the ball would have rebounded out. Such, I guess, are the margins of success and failure. But right now I couldn't care less. I felt a mixture of joy and relief that a season which had been such a trial, such an ordeal, had at least ended in triumph.

FRIDAY 27 MAY

Our last gasp victory over Torino hasn't helped the cause of our manager Rino Marchesi. He has been told today that his two-year contract which is just ending will not be renewed. In other words, he's sacked. The news didn't come as a shock exactly, his job had been in jeopardy for several months.

But I can't help feeling sorry for him as a good, decent and kindly man, even if we did have major differences in our ideas on how the game should be played. Managing Juventus must be one of the toughest jobs in the whole footballing world.

In football at the highest level it's the manager who becomes the fall guy when things go wrong.

To really succeed there, a manager would have to be as tough and bloody-minded as Brian Clough and have a diplomat's tongue as well! The fruits of success can be enormous, the financial rewards nothing short of fabulous. But it's a life in a pressure cooker ... which could explode at any time.

· ELEVEN ·

Playing with Fire

WEDNESDAY 1 JUNE: VALETTA

A day that will rank among the proudest of my life as I captain Wales for the first time. It might not be the grandest occasion ... a friendly match in Malta, with around 10,000 supporters to watch.

But for me it's the fulfilment of a lifetime's ambition. Every little kid who plays football wants to play for his home town team, then for a big club, then for his country and, ultimately, to captain them. So I feel fit to burst with pride as I lead the team out.

Terry Yorath now installed officially as Welsh manager had asked me the previous Sunday night, when the squad assembled at our hotel near Heathrow Airport, if I would like to be captain for the trip. I mightn't have shown much reaction to him as I said yes. But inside, my heart was pumping with excitement.

Kevin Ratcliffe, our regular captain, was absent through injury as was his stand-in Peter Nicholas. Having roomed with Kevin on so many trips, I had a good idea of what was involved. But I wasn't very pleased when Terry took me aside again a little later and told me exactly what he expected from me.

'You've got to show a sense of responsibility. You've got to be captain on and off the pitch. You're a senior pro and the younger ones all look up to you, they'll follow your lead,' he said.

I thought for a moment about giving up the job before I'd started. I didn't see myself as some kind of father-figure, rounding up the lads at night and telling them it was time for bed! But I eventually saw the wisdom of the manager's words.

On a tour like this – we're also playing Italy next Saturday – you have to have someone in the role of players' leader. I just decided to try and set an example.

In our dressing room before the game, though, I've been going round all the players, geeing them up, telling them there is no such thing as a 'friendly' game any more. And that they would need to be at their very best, that there are no easy games against even the smaller nations. The Maltese proved it, leading 2–1 at half time – Barry Horne had scored our first half goal.

Mark Hughes put us level early in the second half. And I managed to nick the winner to give us a 3–2 victory. Clayton Blackmore sent over a high cross which left their goalkeeper undecided whether to come for it or remain on his line. In the end he found himself stranded in no-man's-land as I headed it past him.

THURSDAY 2 JUNE: MILAN AIRPORT

The Welsh party are on their way to Brescia for the second game of our tour against Italy – at least half of us are! We were all together for the flight from Malta to Rome earlier in the day, but seven of the players have somehow managed to miss the shuttle up to Milan.

We discovered later that they went to the wrong terminal and were actually about to board a flight to Chicago when they realized their mistake! It meant they had to catch the next plane up to Milan, four hours later. In the meantime the rest of us are stuck at Milan Airport.

As I'm the only one with any Italian money, I had to buy all the sandwiches and drinks for those who were there. That's carrying the captain's job too far.... But at least we were able to see the funny side of it and we got in a couple of hours' sunbathing in the car park while we waited.

When we all finally meet up, we have an hour and a half's coach ride to our hotel in Brescia. The next day, after we'd trained in the morning, Terry Yorath told us we could spend the afternoon on a trip to Lake Garda. After all the problems of the previous day, he wanted to get us relaxed and we did, too!

We booked a couple of boats and travelled in style round the lake, just like tourists. Afterwards we found a smashing little pavement cafe and sunk a few beers each. 'The Italians will be all wrapped up in bed by now,' I told the lads.

What they would have made of our behaviour I shudder to think. They were expecting to hammer us in any event. They had a good young team who had qualified for the European Championship finals and were expected to get even better in time for the 1990 World Cup.

Before I left Turin, Juventus players were holding up five fingers at me, the number of goals they were forecasting Italy to win by. It wasn't just in fun, either, certainly not by a few of them. They really wanted to see Wales thrashed. But all that did was to make me even more fiercely determined to shock them.

SATURDAY 4 JUNE: BRESCIA

I've just had a telephone call from Francesco Morini telling me I have to be in Turin by seven o'clock the next morning to travel eight hours in a coach to play in a friendly match that night.

I was just about to play for Wales, it would be midnight before I could even leave for the couple of hours drive to Turin. I didn't have the keys to my apartment – Tracy was back home in North Wales – and even if I got to the game I'd be totally drained.

Morini persisted, saying the president had ordered me to turn up. 'If you'd told me a few days earlier I could have organized something. But now, at this kind of notice, it's impossible. I'm already booked on the plane home with Wales tomorrow morning and that's where I'm going,' I told him.

It was hardly the perfect way to prepare for a game. But I was so wound up for this one, it barely made any difference to me. In the Welsh dressing room I'm really pumping up the other players, telling them how much pride was at stake, how the Italians had already dismissed us as little more than fodder.

A capacity 30,000 crowd gave me a lot of stick when I led the team out. But that was nothing to the stick the Italian team dished out in the first twenty minutes. Poor Mark Hughes had studmarks on his calf after one tackle which left his sock hanging almost in two.

We decided that the only answer was to take them on at their own game. So we got stuck in just as hard as they'd been. And then came the magic moment when we scored on the half-hour.

Pat Van Den Hauwe flicked on a long throw-in and I got to the ball before my marker to slide it into the corner of the net with my left foot. I actually got a few cheers from an otherwise stunned crowd, because some supporters had travelled from Turin to back me!

But the goal really caused the Italians to lose their tempers. The game became a brutal war, with players being hacked down if they dared try to hold on to the ball. We were no angels, I admit that. But they were going mad with frustration. Hughes was taking unmerciful punishment. One punch in the face left him with a corker of a black eye. But he's so brave and so strong he never winced and never let them intimidate him.

We held on despite the battering to score a win that was the sweetest in my whole season. But even then the Italian's couldn't take it. I went to shake hands with Gianini at the end and he angrily pushed my hand aside. 'You don't play fair. Wait until next year when you come to Roma ...' he said.

I found his attitude pathetic. I'd been bruised and battered, but once the game's over the least you do is to shake hands. If you still feel angry, then say nothing. But I hope I'm never as petulant as that.

Not that I cared overmuch. I was just thrilled to show the Italians – the game was on television – that I had not forgotten how to score goals. That I still had something left, even if by now the newspapers had decided I'd lost the art of striking.

Morini came to see me in our dressing room afterwards, to ask me once again if I would travel to Turin early the next morning. Again I told him no; it was just impossible. I was going home to North Wales in the morning and returning to Turin on Monday, along with Tracy. I would explain myself to Boniperti then why I could not make that friendly game – which incidentally, Juventus won about 8–0.

TUESDAY 7 JUNE

I'm ready to start my summer break tomorrow, feeling happier than I have for a long time. I've just had a long meeting with Mr Agnelli, who has assured me that I'm still very much wanted by Juventus. They are even planning to bring in one or two more British players to join me.

I'd met the president, Boniperti, the day before, but I saved all my important remarks for today, when I was with the two of them. I explained how disappointed I had been about the season just gone, how I felt the team were not playing to my strengths, not creating the openings.

I also told them of the loneliness I felt in our dressing room, of how some of the players resented me and had deliberately set out to show it. Boniperti said I was wrong, that I was popular among the rest of the squad. 'I can only give you my opinion, how I feel,' I answered.

I told them that although I was happy to stay and see out my contract, I could understand it if they felt they wanted to sell me and bring in somebody new. But Mr Agnelli brushed such talk away, insisting: 'We very much want you to stay. We still have total confidence in you.'

It was then he asked me about British players, who I would like to see in the Juventus team with me. I mentioned Peter Beardsley, John Barnes, Ray Houghton, Steve McMahon, Mark Hughes and Graeme Sharp. I would have been delighted to see any of those joining us.

He's certainly a man of instant action, the owner of Juventus. I was delighted to hear that within a few days they had made a bid for Beardsley which was turned down, then a joint bid for Houghton and McMahon which Liverpool again refused, then they even made a cheeky offer for Hughes, who had just rejoined Manchester United.

For now, though, I was just pleased that he was still

showing his faith in me. He even told the newspapers: 'I want to build my team around Rush next season.' And he promised me that we would be a much more positive, attack-minded team from now on.

Dino Zoff, the legendary former goalkeeper of Juventus and Italy, had taken over from Marchesi as manager. 'He is much more attacking in his ideas,' said Agnelli. That was enough for me. I could enjoy my summer, knowing that things would be so much different from this moment on. I was even impressed with Zoff when I met him briefly. He seemed a nice enough guy and a man with his own mind.

Things were looking up at last. I felt so much better for laying all my cards on the table to our owner, I felt good that he was standing by me. And I'd grown up in this past season.

Both Tracy and myself had learned so much, experienced so much, we'd become so much older and wiser. We would enjoy our summer holiday, then go back to Italy with a totally different and fresh outlook. I wasn't going to take any nonsense any more.

I'd begun to understand the Italian mentality as well as their football and their language. Nice guys come a distant second over here. If you don't stand up for yourself, nobody will. As for the playing side, I know I had a disappointing season, but not nearly as bad as the newspapers have screamed.

I scored fourteen goals all told, which was only four fewer than Maradona, the First Division's leading scorer, and he had something like four penalties in his total as well. But the difference is that only eight of mine have come in the League, the rest were all scored in cup competitions. Over here, unlike England, the League is the *only* thing that matters.

· TWELVE ·

No Place Like Home

The first day of pre-season training for Juventus and here am I hardly able to walk, let alone think about kicking a football. I'm a hell of a lot stronger than I was a couple of weeks ago, mind, but still getting over an illness that left me lower, more drained, than I ever thought possible.

It started at the beginning of the month, in the final couple of days of our holiday in the Cayman Islands. I had what I thought were heat lumps beginning to appear all over my body, so I put extra suntan cream on them. But by the time it came to fly home I was in agony.

Tracy called the doctor in as soon as we arrived back at her parents' home, where we were staying. He immediately diagnosed a bout of chickenpox. Putting on that cream instead of the correct lotion had only served to aggravate the illness.

I'd also somehow contrived to catch a mild dose of hepatitis and shingles, as well as a liver infection. It all combined to leave me in a total, tormented fever for five days. I didn't eat a thing and I don't think I slept more than ten minutes at a time, the pain was so intense.

I even asked the doctor if there was someting he could give me to knock me out for a few days. 'There's nothing that can be done. You'll just have to put up with the agony for three or four more days,' he said. I did. By the end of it I was completely exhausted, as weak as a kitten.

I saw a specialist who told me that I would need several weeks of rest and recuperation, to build up my strength before I could even think of going back to Italy. I'd lost more than eight pounds in weight and there's not that much spare flesh on my body.

I telephoned Juventus, to explain what had happened. But I think they believed I was just being difficult and wanting a longer holiday, especially after what had happened after my Christmas break. They sent their club doctor across to see me and even he was stunned when he saw how ill I was.

He told me there was no question of my getting back to Italy until I was much stronger. Yet within a day or two of him returning, I had a call from the club telling me they wanted me over there as soon as possible.

I went back to the local specialist, who told me once again that I could forget about travelling for another few weeks at least. But right now I'm torn about what to do. I really feel far from well, but I know that there will already be whispers in Turin that I'm pulling a fast one again.

FRIDAY 29 JULY: LUCERNE

They say the Swiss mountain air is the healthiest in the world. You could have fooled me! I've just been for a walk around the hills and I'm knackered. I'd flown here earlier in the day to join my team-mates, who have been at the training camp for nearly a week now.

The specialist back in Wales had advised me to remain at home for a further week at least. But I had to get over here, to show everybody that I really am determined to play my part for Juventus this season. I still feel far from well and I know I look ill, but there are still those who are sceptical.

For the next couple of days, it's as much as I can do to take a brisk walk, breathing in the air. I still couldn't eat properly. But within a few days, the doctor has me jogging gently. I still couldn't think of kicking a ball and I hadn't touched one when the team played a match against a local side and we headed back to Italy.

We went straight to Villa Perosa, where we trained for a couple more days. By now I was feeling a fair bit stronger so I joined in the running with the rest of the players. But it left me exhausted. On the morning of the game between the senior team and the reserves I felt so drained I went up to my room and just lay on the bed for more than two hours.

Nobody even bothered to come up and check if I was all right or needed some attention. I could have been dying for all they knew. Maybe I was being a bit too suspicious, but it struck me as being a bit off.

We'd signed a couple of new players in the close season – veteran Italian international Altobelli and a Portuguese midfielder called Rui Barros. I must say that Altobelli seems a great bloke, he's been more friendly towards me in a week or so than most of the others were in a year.

So that's encouraging, although I'm disappointed we were not able to sign any of the British players I'd talked about with Agnelli. Then the club announce they're going to sign Russian star Zavarov. That means four overseas players, counting Laudrup and myself and, with only three allowed to play in each team, somebody has to go.

In fact, Laudrup was already resigned to being on his way. Juventus had agreed terms with PSV Eindhoven for his

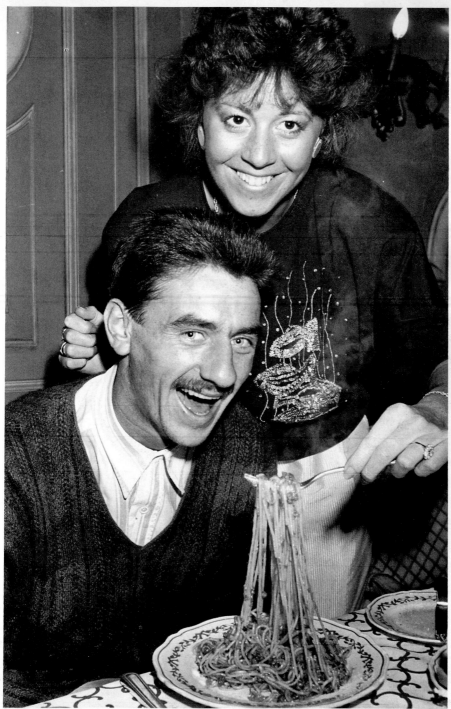

How Tracey pasta test in the kitchen.

Determined, as I take the field against Avellino.

Getting to grips with the Italian game.

My first League goal – what a relief!

(*Right*) Wired for sound? No, just passing my medical at Juventus.
(*Below*) Rino Marchesi faces another grilling from the Italian press.

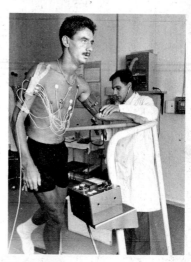

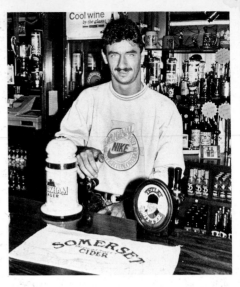

Home for Christmas – with real beer at last . . .

. . . and ready for a kick-about with my brothers (left to right) Peter, Graham and Stephen.

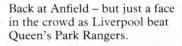

Back at Anfield – but just a face in the crowd as Liverpool beat Queen's Park Rangers.

On the international scene. Shaking hands with the great Ruud Gullit on the day I captained my country against Holland.

Celebrating a goal for Wales with Mark Hughes.

Liverpool vs. an England XI. It felt like I'd never been away. In the Liverpool line up (left to right) Bruce Grobbelaar, Gary Ablett, Nigel Spackman, Craig Johnston, Steve McMahon, me, John Aldridge, Jan Molby and John Barnes.

My second goal of the match – it's nice to prove I haven't lost my touch.

The Boss seems pleased
with my efforts.

The wanderer returns.

Back in action for the Reds.

There's no place like it.

transfer and he was actually discussing his move with them. He had been moping around, far from excited at the prospect. So I wasn't totally surprised when the move broke down. But I was stunned, dumbfounded, by what followed. . . .

SATURDAY 13 AUGUST

I'm back in my apartment settling down for the evening after training when I get the phone call that is going to transform my life again. Paul Dean, my advisor, is on the end of the line, speaking from England. His words are buzzing in my ears: 'Would you be interested in going back to Liverpool . . .?'

At first I think it's all a joke. Then, when he repeats the question, I begin to realize he's being deadly serious. 'I'm all right here,' was my initial reaction. Then I paused to think about the situation. He explained that Juventus had given Liverpool permission to talk to me.

Things never stay the same for long in football. Nobody is indispensable. Liverpool, as professional as ever, had noticed their problem with four foreign players. And as soon as the Laudrup move broke down they pounced, at a moment when Juventus were facing embarrassment.

My hand is trembling on the phone, a thousand thoughts rampaging through my mind, as Paul continues to talk. Despite all my troubles, despite all the talk in the newspapers about my being unsettled and unhappy, I really had set my mind on at least another year in Italy.

But my heart is beating faster, the adrenalin pumping at the very notion of going back home, pulling on that red Liverpool shirt again. Tracy and I talk it over for a long time. She knows that when it comes to a decision on football, the choice must be mine. She's happy to go along with whatever I want.

MONDAY 15 AUGUST

Peter Robinson calls me to say that Juventus are prepared to let me go. I've had two days – and two sleepless nights – to take a stronger grasp of the situation by now. I know I have to go.

Clearly, the Italians have made up their minds that they can do without me. In fact, Robinson reveals that the two clubs have already agreed a deal by telephone. It was done with such lightning speed because of the special bond of trust between them ... the one decent legacy of the horror of Heysel.

I tell him that I have made up my mind, that I want to come back. He's delighted but also concerned, in case the story should be leaked to the newspapers. 'We don't want a single soul to know anything until the moment you arrive back here,' he told me.

So I can't even tell my mum and dad or Tracy's parents. It is so difficult, bursting to tell the world that Rushie's on his way back to Anfield, yet sworn to absolute secrecy. Never mind. I'm only going to have to keep quiet for a couple of days at the most.

It gives me time, too, to think about the implications of going back. The prospect of playing alongside my old mates again was really exciting and linking up with the newer players, like John Barnes and Peter Beardsley, would be great.

I'd watched Liverpool play the previous season and knew they were still a tremendous team. Yet there would be difficulties ahead, too. After all their fabulous success last season, it was an impossible act to follow. They were not going to go twenty-nine games unbeaten again this time. No team can.

There would also be a lot of personal pressure on me. People would automatically assume that I'm going to return to the First Division in a blaze of glory, score fifty goals. I know that's ridiculous, but it still won't stop them expecting it or giving me stick if I don't start scoring goals right from the start.

But what the hell! After all the slagging I'd taken from the Italian press, I'm hardened to face up to anything. I'm going to a club that want me – that's what is important. They wanted me badly enough to pay back most of the £3.2 million Juventus had paid them for me just a year ago. That was enough for me.

WEDNESDAY 17 AUGUST

Now I'm really on my way! Paul Dean has been across to help me sort out my affairs with Juventus. Now that I'm leaving, they seem to have lost all interest in me. I didn't see Boniperti, only one of his colleagues. But at least we are parting on amicable terms.

I don't see why we shouldn't, though. After all, I never expected to be leaving. It was a bolt out of the blue when it worked out that way.

They also told me that there was never any danger of any other club moving in with a last gasp bid for me. Everton, Manchester United and Rangers had all asked Juventus to be kept informed if there ever was the possibility of me leaving. Newcastle United and Tottenham had also been linked. But they were all wasting their time.

'If you don't join Liverpool, then you must stay with Juventus,' I was told. The warning was totally unnecessary. By that time I'd already made up my mind that if I did leave, Liverpool were the only British club I would have joined.

Anyway, it will all be over tomorrow. I'm flying over to Manchester to complete the signing. In the meantime, I'm having to go about my daily business as if nothing is happening. That's next to impossible when you want to scream out the news.

By now, I realize I just *have* to let our families know, to save them the acute shock when the story breaks tomorrow. So I phoned my dad, pledging him not to say a word to a soul and Tracey told her parents, with the same warning.

THURSDAY 18 AUGUST: MANCHESTER

Kenny Dalglish has met me at the airport and now we're off in his car to a medical examination and then a press conference that has already had British football buzzing. Reporters and photographers are there anticipating a costly new signing but they're still not quite sure exactly who.

I felt at ease with Kenny straight away, as he cracked a few jokes and made me relax, just as if the last year had never happened. It's nice to feel wanted again and its marvellous to attend a press conference where all the questions are asked and answered in English! I was there for what seemed an eternity, with television and radio interviews to conduct as well.

The medical test is a formality. But I know that, as for fitness, I'm a long way behind the other players. They've already done all the hard pre-season grind. They're playing in the Charity Shield at Wembley in just a couple of days.

I've got a lot of catching up to do in that respect. But it still doesn't prevent the tremble of excitement I feel inside me. 'Words can't describe how I feel right now ...' I had told the pressmen. 'This is the best club in the world. They have a great squad and I only hope I can help.'

FRIDAY 19 AUGUST: LIVERPOOL

Now I really feel like I've never been away. I'm back in the changing room, where I've been given my old space. I've got a new neighbour, though, in John Barnes and what a livewire he is already, full of wisecracks.

The lads have all welcomed me back, telling me they were staggered when the news broke on the radio yesterday afternoon. The papers are already speculating that John Aldridge's days are numbered, that he will have to give up his first team place to me.

But we've been good pals since he joined the club and his welcome seems as genuine as anybody's. Who's to say what's in the manager's mind? I know that I'm a long, long way from match fitness, that it's going to be weeks before I feel strong enough to play. Who knows what will happen in the meantime?

As for the supporters, though, they have been struck by what one newspaper called 'Rush-Mania'. More than five hundred season tickets have been sold today – twelve times the normal daily rate. 'We haven't had a day like this for years,' said the club's assistant secretary Roy Jones. Peter Robinson says: 'The Rush interest is phenomenal. It's just a pity we don't have a bigger ground!' Even two hundred and fifty miles away in London, where Liverpool open their league season against Charlton at Selhurst Park the next weekend, ticket sales are reported to have soared after my signing.

Yet there's no way I'll be ready to even play there. Having missed all the pre-season training and struggled to get back my strength after my summer illness, I have a lot of hard work to do at the training ground before I can count myself fit.

I still have things to organize for our move back home.

Tracy and I are off to Turin in the morning to tie up all the loose ends and start packing. It's amazing how much furniture we've accumulated, even in the short space of time we've been married. Now we're going to have to find a house to put it all in.

MONDAY 22 AUGUST

This time it really is Arrivederci Italy – for good. Tracy is staying on for a few more days to supervise the removal men when they arrive. But I'm flying back today to get down to the job of being a Liverpool player again.

The local newspapers have sent me off with a typical farewell gesture, saying how the club would be better without me. Yet the fans in the street have all wished me the best of luck, they hold no hostility towards me. I'll never have a word said against the vast majority of Juventus' supporters, as far as I'm concerned they've been brilliant.

Yet, as I sit for a while and reflect on the past twelve months, I have to say I never felt part of Juventus. If I'd been there one year or five years, it would have made no difference. I'd have still felt like an outsider, with no real ties to the club.

Not that I regret moving here. It has been a fascinating experience, one which helped me to grow up and set me up for life financially. It's also given me an insight into life in a country where everyone is totally wrapped up in football, where it's the highlight of their lives.

Everybody, but *everybody*, is an expert. From the waiter at the restaurant to the doorman at the hotel, they all know exactly what's wrong with the team, and what they don't know they insist on hearing from you! They read the sports pages avidly and believe everything that's written.

That makes the press almighty. Much too powerful and much too demanding. They want to know every little aspect of your personal life, let alone what you do on the pitch; and what they don't know they promptly make up. The things I'm supposed to have done would make you blush.

I've been drunk in nightclubs and discos, with a girl on each arm ... I've been legless through drink on the night before a match ... I've indulged in wild, high-speed car races through the streets at midnight ... I've been a hermit, who never goes out, shuns the social life and sits at home eating baked beans ... and I've given Tracy a right good hiding every few weeks when she's complained!

Yep, it's been one helluva time. I must be mad to even consider coming home after a lifestyle like that! But seriously, those wild stories are devoured and believed by so many people and that's when it stops being funny.

I could have put up with all that, though, if I'd been happy in my work. That's where the real problem lay. I became so lonely, felt so alone and left out in the Juventus dressing room my life there in the end became nothing better than purgatory.

Maybe I should have been more demonstrative when I first arrived, swaggered around like a superstar. They might have reacted more to that. Italy is a country where everything's exaggerated, where the louder you shout the more people take notice.

But that's not my style. I tried to break myself in gradually. But they take everything on face value. If they decide you're quiet and shy, they'll steamroller over you. They'll treat you like dirt and ignore you.

I just felt left out of everything. Bruno, Brio and Tacconi were brilliant. Perhaps a few more friendly words from the others would have made all the difference. It just got me down, left me feeling empty.

There were days when the despair and depression became so overpowering I was sorely tempted to get back to the apartment, pack a suitcase and clear off back to England. Instead, I'd take it out on Tracy, who had to put up with my moods and listen to my problems. I guess when you're unhappy at work, it's always the wife who suffers.

Humour in the dressing room is the one thing that I missed so much playing in Italian football. If those players could see me at Liverpool, laughing and joking with my team-mates, they wouldn't believe it – actually enjoying myself is all-important to me.

I don't ever recall sharing a dressing room joke, enjoying the banter there. It just wasn't me to be sitting there without a smile and that, in a nutshell, is why Juventus never saw the real Ian Rush. If I'm happy with my life, then I play well. It's as simple as that.

If I'm miserable, then it will affect my game. When I look back at it all now, I can't remember too many laughs. All I remember is a vague feeling of unease every time I walked into the dressing room.

There was never anything tangible, just an atmosphere, enough to make you sense that you were not wanted there and that can be more cruel than any physical battering. In fact, I'd have been almost relieved to have a slanging match or even a punch-up. That at least would have brought things into the open.

I never got to understand the running of the club. As far as I could see, things weren't organized along the lines I had come to know at Liverpool. At Anfield everyone had their own job from the manager to the tea lady. At Juventus things appeared to be more complicated, with a system which I found hard to follow.

Boniperti was a very excitable man who obviously enjoyed day-to-day contact with everyone at the club. He clearly

demanded absolute loyalty and loved to show his appreci-
ation for hard work and excellence.

Marchesi was perhaps too much of a gentleman to stand
up for himself. The papers were always carrying stories of
our bust-ups, but I can never once remember him having a
go at me. In fact I felt sorry for him because I know the
players disliked him.

They would be two-faced with him, talking nicely to him
one minute then stabbing him in the back. He carried the
can for our relatively poor season by being dismissed. Yet I
certainly don't put all the blame down to him for he never
had a free hand.

But one man I will miss is Agnelli, the owner. If I was
ready to play for anyone at Juventus it was him. To repay
him for the faith and loyalty he had always shown in me. I
have a lot of affection for him and, knowing how much it
burns inside him to make the club great again, I am certain
he will get it right eventually.

It might take until after the World Cup, which is staged
in Italy in 1990. But you watch what happens then. Juventus
will pocket the best foreign players in the finals and they'll
snatch all the best Italians too. They'll get them because they
have an owner to whom money is absolutely no object in the
pursuit of success. Because, in spite of my experiences there,
they remain the greatest club in Italy.

I would never try to put another British player off, if he
had the chance to sample the Italian experience. Go, I would
tell them. Go for the financial rewards, for the experience.
But go there with a swagger, with an arrogance. Tell them
all how good you are, how you will take Italian football
by storm. They'll all believe it as the people are very easily
led.

Learn the language, be prepared for all the niggling tactics
of opponents on the field. But most of all understand their

mentality. Remember, they would prefer to believe what they hear and what they read rather than what they actually see. So, in a sentence, give them plenty of bullshit!

· THIRTEEN ·

Postscript

WEDNESDAY 12 OCTOBER: WALSALL

Maybe it wasn't the most spectacular goal I ever scored. But for sheer relief, the one I've just tucked away will take some beating. It might have been against a side just fresh from the Third Division – but it's still a mighty psychological barrier I've just overcome.

It's my first since I returned to Liverpool and the fact that the season is nearly two months old shows there's been something radically wrong with me. I've played ten games without a goal and it's been shades of Italy, as the British press have slaughtered me. What they seem to have conveniently overlooked is that in half those games I only played a substitute's role – sometimes no more than ten or twenty minutes.

But they had all forecast that I would come home in style, smash forty goals, and that Liverpool would be invincible. I knew it was ridiculous. I was nowhere near match fitness when I returned and because I was so desperate to play for Liverpool, I came into the side too quickly.

I thought I needed match-practice to get me fit, but that

was wrong. What I had needed was rest and recuperation. I'd feel totally drained after every game, I suffered severe headaches – frankly, I was washed out. On top of all that, we were living out of our suitcases at Tracy's parents' home and we had to readjust to Britain again: the food, the climate, things like that.

The manager, Kenny Dalglish, has done a lot to keep my confidence from falling with my lack of goals. 'Take no notice of anybody else. It's what we think at the club that counts, and we have total belief in you – the goals will flow again before long,' he told me.

The problems all came to a head last month, when I played in three tough games in the space of a week. It began with Wales playing a World Cup tie against Holland in Amsterdam. Mark Hughes and myself were given very demanding roles, involving a lot of running and harrying, to stop the Dutch from organizing those sweeping attacks from their back four.

I was captain again that night, and it was nice to shake hands with Ruud Gullit the Dutch skipper, who told me: 'Good luck on going back to Liverpool, I'm sure it is the right move for you.' But it was Gullit who finally beat us that night, with a header just nine minutes from the end.

Afterwards I felt more exhausted than I ever had in my life. But it was straight back home to face Tottenham the following weekend, then a Mercantile Credit Cup game at Arsenal the following Tuesday. I could hardly walk by then. I even saw the Liverpool doctor, who told me that I was suffering from the stress of all that had happened since my summer illness.

Fortunately, things have started to sort themselves out since then. We've found a beautiful house, tucked away in the Wirral, which we're moving into shortly. While Tracy's parents have been great, it will still be nice to be in our own home again.

Last weekend at Luton, although we lost 1–0, I felt that my sharpness was finally back. For the first time, there were no headaches or aches and pains afterwards. My general play was good again, I was running well and my touch was back. I came off that plastic surface just *knowing* that I'd score at Walsall tonight.

The goal came in the second half, when I picked up a pass with my back to goal, turned and just hit it low past their goalkeeper. It helped us to a 3–1 win. 'About time,' was all I could say to myself as it went in.

Now, with my confidence flowing again, I'm out to get twenty goals this season. I won't regard that as any great achievement, it won't be a vintage season for me. But just watch out – next season I'll be better than ever. My target is forty goals then. Then those who have been hounding me will have to eat their words. I hope that's not sounding boastful, but it is something I honestly feel inside. If you don't believe in your own ability, you might as well pack the game in altogether.

It has been a hit and miss start to the season for Liverpool but that was inevitable after their incredible run of success last year. Right now Norwich are on top of the First Division, while the whole country seems to be talking about Arsenal as the team to break the Merseyside monopoly on the Championship.

I've seen Arsenal at first hand, and they are a good, positive side, with players playing to the limit of their skills. But if you ask me who is going to win the title, there is still only one honest answer for me – Liverpool.

We've had a terrible run of early season injuries, the manager has had to make do and mend where he can. But we're still only a few points off the top and that despite the inevitable speculation that Liverpool are in the midst of a crisis! Wait until the new year, when we'll be back to something approaching full strength. Watch us go then.

Meantime it's still the best club in the whole world to me. It always will be. I'm even more proud than ever to pull on that red shirt, prouder than I ever was to wear the blue and white of Juventus. Everyone's so down to earth, there's no place for any bigheads here. Come to think of it, it mightn't be a bad thing for a few Italians to come and play for Liverpool. Maybe then they'd learn that football is a team game not just a platform for individuals. . . .

· FOURTEEN ·

My Story – Tracy Rush

There are some precious moments which will live in your memory forever. I will never forget the look on Ian's face when he answered that first telephone call to tell him that Liverpool were ready to bring him back home.

His face lit up, there was a happiness, an excitement about him that had not been there throughout his whole season with Juventus. I knew at that moment that he had to take the chance to come back, I was so pleased for him. I would have liked him to have made a success over there before leaving and I really believe that he would have done so this season.

Yet it used to break my heart to see him as low and depressed as he had been. I'd never seen him like that before – he was cracking jokes from the night I first met him eight years ago. Now, to see him so sad and unhappy was terribly upsetting.

Day after day he would come home from training aching with loneliness. 'You don't know what it's like going into that dressing room and having people ignore you,' he would say. 'I know you get lonely at home but at least you can hide away from people if you want. I've got to go and face them every day. I'd rather be on my own than with people who just don't want to know you.'

The situation was bound to lead to friction between us at times. I would tell him not to be so thin-skinned, to snap out of his mood and then be sorry for what I'd said. But I was being hurt too, in a different way. I felt so much for him, and his unhappiness only made me miserable as well.

I must say that at first I thought he was exaggerating the situation. But it really struck home to me when we went to the club's Christmas party. Apart from one or two, the other players turned their backs on him and did not even say a word. It was terrible. I could understand then just how much he had been suffering, having this kind of treatment day in day out.

Ian's problem is that he has always been basically quite shy and he has no conceit at all. At Liverpool they deliberately play down the 'superstar' image, but in Italy things are different. Footballers at famous clubs enjoy all the trappings of stardom – with the publicity and attention that go with it.

Ian is exactly the opposite. He will always shun the bright lights, preferring to melt into the background rather than hold the centre stage. He likes to enjoy himself but the one thing I have honestly never seen him do is act like a superstar.

It's the Italian mentality which is the hardest thing to learn over there – much more difficult even than the language. Yet, looking back on it all now, neither of us will ever regret the experience. We've both grown up a lot, learned to stand on our own two feet, and it's made us financially secure. We do have some treasured memories, some true friends over there.

I had been worried for a whole year before we went. Getting married and then moving to a new country – how was I going to be able to manage? Yet the forebodings were far worse than the actual reality. I actually settled down a lot quicker than Ian.

I had worked hard at learning the language before we went, enough at least to get by, to buy goods and food in the shops, things like that. We both went to college in Liverpool once a week to study Italian. But Ian would never do his homework. He'd just look at the phrase book for about five minutes before each lesson! In the end I gave up trying to goad him into doing the work.

I did have a lot more spare time than him. By now I'd given up my job in a bank, so I was able to devote far more time towards studying. To be fair to Ian, he really worked hard at the language once we actually arrived there and, contrary to what a lot of people believe, he could speak it quite fluently by the time we left.

The thing I found most difficult to come to terms with in Turin was driving. I thought I'd never have the courage to even take a car onto those streets, teeming with maniacs whose only idea of driving was apparently to go as fast and as recklessly as they could!

Then one day Ian brought home a car for me. So I summoned up some nerve and drove it into the city to do some shopping. We were living only a couple of miles outside, so it took about five minutes to get there. It took me two hours, though, to get back! I took a wrong turn and that was it. Ian laughed and said: 'In future, just head towards the hills, until you spot a familiar landmark.' So that was what I did from then on.

Being in a strange country, so far from your family and friends, made it terribly lonely at times, especially when Ian was away. I was lucky to strike up a friendship with Michael Laudrup's girlfriend Tina. Like me she was far from home and was also lonely. So we spent a lot of time together, going shopping, going to each other's houses for meals and going to many of the home games together.

The wives of players like Bruno, Brio and Tacconi were also very friendly. But I was given a helpful piece of advice. 'I'll tell you now, you're better to make friends away from football. There's so much talking behind backs at Italian football clubs.'

Cristina Morini, wife of one of the Juventus backroom staff, was a great help when I first moved to Turin. It was Cristina who first introduced me to Tina and Cristina who came with my mum and myself when we went to choose where to live.

We had three or four different places to visit and I finished up making the biggest mistake I ever made in Italy . . . despite having a premonition that it was wrong. The three of us all agreed that one apartment was outstandingly the best. It was breathtakingly beautiful, with glorious views, lovely gardens.

But I wasn't very keen on the owner, a Mr Lucca, who would live with his family on the ground floor while Ian and I would live on the top floor. 'I love the place but I'm not sure about that man. He's just not my type,' I told the others. I think they knew what I meant. But it was such a lovely place to live, I decided to take Ian along before we made a final decision.

This time, of course, Lucca was politeness itself. Ian thought I'd been imagining things! 'Nothing wrong with the fella at all,' he said. So we decided to rent the apartment and for a couple of months the landlord was pleasant enough. But he finished up causing fifty per cent of our problems and, though usually I get on with all sorts, we just couldn't hit it off.

Lucca was obviously an important businessman in Turin and he was really excited to know a famous footballer. He wanted to introduce Ian to all his friends and business associates. He wanted to take us here and there all the time, meeting this 'important man' and that one.

At first it was nice enough, but we eventually found that our lives were not our own. It really got on Ian's nerves. He's just not the kind to be stage-managed in that way. I used to have to push him, to say we'll have to accept Lucca's invitations now and then, just to keep the peace.

He was always insisting on taking me to all the home games, but that made me feel under pressure. It seemed an imposition. But when he realized that we just wanted to run our own lives he appeared very put out. We were not helped when stories began appearing in the Italian newspapers about how Ian used to beat me up, that he used to stay away from home all night, that we had terrible slanging matches. It was quite a contrast to earlier stories . . . that we never went out, shunned the world, and sat at home every night eating baked beans!

The worst story of all came towards the end of our year there, when it was alleged in the newspapers that Ian had been bashing me about so violently that the whole house was shaking. It was alleged that Mr Lucca's stepson became so afraid that he ran out of the house.

The truth of the matter is that Ian is just not the type to hit a woman – any woman. I know that for a fact. I've given him a clip from time to time, when my temper has boiled over, but he's never so much as raised a hand against me.

These stories about the constant friction at home got back to the club. I was getting the blame for Ian not playing as well as he could. It was all nonsense, but Boniperti eventually asked to see me. 'I know the problems of settling into a new country, but you really must encourage Ian. You must understand his problems,' he told me.

Lucca was so incensed when we told him we were leaving, to return to Liverpool, that he actually tried to charge us an extra two years' rent. He threatened to lock the removal van in the grounds of the house until we paid. It gave him quite a shock when the van arrived from England in just a few days. He didn't think it could be organized so quickly. Ian had already returned to Liverpool by then, so I supervised the removal on my own.

It was a shame, because I liked the Italian people. You have to accept and understand their different approach to life, but the everyday person in the street is smashing. I went on an Italian language crash course at an adult class and learned quickly. The teacher would have us all taking turns to speak in front of the whole class and if you hadn't done your homework, you'd look stupid.

I quickly got over my embarrassment at speaking in Italian to the local people, even if I made mistakes. I remember just before we left, I was telling Bruno and his wife about Ian's illness. I meant to tell them he had been suffering from chickenpox but the equivalent word in Italian is very similar to the word for wine. They suddenly burst out laughing while I was talking – I'd got the two words mixed up.

The fans were always so kind and considerate. But watching Ian play was certainly different to the days at Liverpool. My stand seat happened to be right in the middle of a crowd of men, who quickly got to know who I was. Whenever Ian scored a goal, I'd have people coming up to shake my hand, hug me and even lift me up and swing me round! There were times when I wondered if it was him or me who had just scored. . . .

Ian and I also had a teacher, Silvana Gill, who taught us at home one afternoon a week. She became a good friend as well as Ian's unofficial secretary, helping with his mail and such like. Silvana loved Turin. She went to stay with her grandmother for a short holiday five years ago – and has been there ever since!

When we were out together, for a meal or whatever, supporters used to come up and ask me for *my* autograph. It was terribly embarrassing, but they would say: 'You are just as famous as him.' Ian wasn't amused, mind. 'Who do you think you are?' he would say. But the fans just wouldn't take no for an answer.

They must have been reading the newspapers and believing what they read. Actually I was only interviewed by the Italian press once – when we went to Turin for the first time, just after Ian had signed. They invented all my answers then and from that stage they used to make up my words without even bothering to ask me.

There was always a description of what I wore to every match ... one report described me as 'having a helmet of red hair and wearing a bottle green suit'. They could hardly get the hair wrong, but I haven't an outfit of that colour to my name. They used to have amazing quotes about what I felt of Ian's performances, his goals. One story told how I had a dog called Rambo and how I needed a washing machine. Don't ask me how ... but the peculiar thing was I did need one at that time!

The newspapers really got the knife into Ian, but the fans really took to him. They were always sympathetic. I think they realized he had joined the club at the wrong time, when the team were not up to their former standard. They knew he had done nothing like as badly as the journalists had made out.

We both became very partial to Italian food as well. One Juventus supporter actually sent me an Italian cookbook, written in English, so I gave it a go; and I became pretty good at cooking pastas – lasagne, spaghetti, things like that.

The weather was another bonus. Spring in Italy is hotter than summer in Britain and the winter was so pleasant, we were actually sunbathing on our balcony in February. But

Turin is hardly the most exciting city in Italy. Whenever friends or family came to stay, we went round the usual haunts – the Shroud of Turin, a lovely park, the automobile museum – and that was it.

I came home to North Wales whenever I could. If Ian was away for a few days, he preferred me to be with my family rather than in the apartment on my own and there were times when I wanted to pack everything in and just come home for good. It was awfully lonely when I was in the house by myself. Things always seemed worse then.

Our telephone bill in the time we were in Italy averaged more than £1,000 a month, which gives some indication of how often we were calling our families and friends back in Britain. When Ian and I were both back in Flint together, among our own folk, it was a real wrench to have to go back to Turin.

Yet, when I look back at it all now, I'm glad we went. We would have spent the rest of our lives wondering otherwise. It's changed our whole attitude to life and I think we are both far more appreciative of living in Britain. We all moan and groan about it, but a year away helps you to realize what a fine country it really is.

We have also grown up a lot, learned a new language, and seen another, very different way of life – you can't put a price on that kind of experience. We have also made ourselves financially secure for life. That is why I would never try to dissuade anybody from going to Italy, or any other foreign country for that matter, to further their careers.

Indeed, to be honest, I had mixed feeling about coming home when the Liverpool move came up. I really believe that if Ian had stayed with Juventus another season, he would have become a hero. By the end of that first year we were both so much older and wiser, we had mastered the language, learned how to 'think' Italian. We went back there for the second season with a totally different attitude.

We were both much more positive. 'Give it another year and if we still feel the same then we'll definitely come back' – that was our philosophy. Ian wasn't going to let any dressing room problems get him down any more. He was going out to do his best and to hell with anything else.

Perhaps his experience on holiday in the Cayman Islands made him realize that nothing could be quite so bad. The place itself was beautiful, but towards the end of the holiday, he came out in all these tiny blisters. We thought it was some kind of heat rash, so he plastered them with suntan cream.

By the time we were due to return home he was really in distress. We were delayed at Miami Airport for five hours and he was just like a zombie; he couldn't even say how ill he felt. He was beginning to fear he had picked up some tropical disease.

I called the doctor as soon as we arrived at my parents home and we found he was suffering from chickenpox. The poor thing had contracted several other infections as well and he was in absolute agony for days and nights on end.

He even woke me up one night and asked: 'Can you die from chickenpox?' It sounds funny now, but at the time I felt so sorry for him. He couldn't even wear normal clothes because they irritated his skin so much, all he could wear was a light tracksuit. He didn't eat a thing for about five days and lost well over half a stone – Ian just hasn't got that kind of spare weight to lose. Even the Juventus doctor, who came to see him, gasped: 'Ian, you look terrible'.

But Juventus still insisted that he should get back over there for training as quickly as possible. He was nowhere near fit, or even well, when he went to join the team in Switzerland. With all the upheaval of his move back to Liverpool following within a few weeks, I don't think he's totally over his illness even now.

Still, what happened on our last night together in Turin might have been its own message that the move back was the right one. We went for a meal in a restaurant, only for my car to be stolen virtually from outside the front door.

Eventually the police rang to report they had found it. It was slightly damaged, but would I like to collect it? I took the car keys with me, expecting to drive it back to the apartment only to discover that the thieves had stolen the wheels, the engine, even the windows and the seats. All that was left inside was the gearstick!

The policeman who called me was very excited and speaking very quickly so I must have missed something in the translation. However, undaunted, I may continue learning Italian, perhaps even taking an O Level. Just to show myself how much I really did learn.

· FIFTEEN ·

Rush – The Verdict

GRAEME SOUNESS: I was disappointed for Ian but not surprised by what happened to him in Italy. His problem was that he chose the right team at the wrong time. There is no question that Juventus are a fabulous club. And Rushie was the best striker of his kind in the world when he joined them. All he needed was the ball in the opposing penalty area – and he would score goals. It was as guaranteed as that.

But from my own time playing in Italy, I knew that Juventus were essentially a counter-attacking team, in which Ian would be expected to forage a lonely road up front. At least in my time, however, they had Michel Platini in their midfield. He was a wonderful passer of the ball, the man to create the openings for Rushie to put away. But when he retired he was never replaced. The result was that Ian was left with little in the way of support or service from his midfield.

Ian's not the George Best type of forward, who can make long, mazy runs with the ball past a trail of defenders. His game is made up of sharp acceleration and an uncanny knack of scoring goals – but no striker, however good he is, can succeed without being given the ball.

PAUL DEAN: The most important consequence of Ian's year in Italy was that it made him grow up. He had been used to a fairly cossetted lifestyle back in Britain and he suddenly found himself in a foreign country, having to speak a different language, having to come to terms with a very different way of looking at things and with the added responsibilities of a young wife.

For probably the first time in his career, he found that life can have its downturns as well. From the time I spent with him in Turin I know that he had a wonderful rapport with the supporters. But, while he had a few close friends at Juventus, he missed the dressing-room banter that was part and parcel of the Liverpool scene.

And the pressmen who hounded him and constantly mis-quoted him really angered and frustrated Ian. The problem was that the Italians, starved of a native film industry or major international pop stars, turn their top soccer players into figures of almost hysterical adulation.

Ian was expected to be as flamboyant off the pitch as he was skilful on it, but that was not his way. Ian is basically a shy person. And this shyness inevitably led him into conflict with a media who demanded a larger-than-life personality.

KEVIN RATCLIFFE: Considering all the problems of settling down to a new life in a strange country, I don't think Ian did at all badly in Italy. But I am convinced that if he had stayed with Juventus another season he would really have become a hero there.

I spoke to him a lot on the telephone while he was in Turin, keeping him in touch with the scene over here. I knew he was having trouble from some of his team-mates. And I knew he was not altogether happy at the way things were going.

But I could sense an extra steely determination about him

as the months went by. Ian was coming to terms with life over there, his attitude was hardening. And he would also have felt less personal pressure in a second season. He would also have been part of a much better team, with the new signings Juventus had made in the summer. Still, he will be wiser – and richer – for the experience.

JAN MOLBY: As a Dane who has played most of his career abroad – with PSV Eindhoven in Holland and now with Liverpool in England – I know it is far from easy to adjust to different countries and different temperaments.

But I was lucky inasmuch that just about everyone in my country is taught English at school. So the language barrier was not so difficult for me to overcome. Also, the players at Liverpool all went out of their way to help me settle down and feel at home.

Ian, in particular, made sure that I never suffered from homesickness. He has been a great friend as well as a great team-mate. Unfortunately, it seems that the players in Juventus, most of them anyway, were anything but helpful towards him. It must be a different mentality, that players in Italy are not so friendly towards outsiders.

It is good for Liverpool to have Rush back. But I remain convinced that in the right team he has the talent to score goals anywhere in the world.